Ethics

Mary Mothersill
BARNARD COLLEGE

Sources in Philosophy
A MACMILLAN SERIES
Lewis White Beck, General Editor
THE MACMILLAN COMPANY
COLLIER–MACMILLAN LIMITED, LONDON

© Copyright, MARY MOTHERSILL, 1965
All rights reserved. No part of this book may be reproduced or utilized in any form or by any means, electronic or mechanical, including photocopying, recording or by any information storage and retrieval system, without permission in writing from the Publisher.
Fourth Printing, 1969
Library of Congress catalog card number: 65-10522
THE MACMILLAN COMPANY
COLLIER-MACMILLAN CANADA, LTD., TORONTO, ONTARIO
Printed in the United States of America

Contents

MARY MOTHERSILL / Introduction … 1

PART I. WHY MEN FIND IT HARD TO DO WHAT IS RIGHT

PLATO / The Myth of Gyges and Natural Justice … 25

JOHN CALVIN / Original Sin and The Human Vocation … 29

ALBERT CAMUS / Encounter with the Absurd … 35

THOMAS HOBBES / Of the State of Men Without Civil Society … 41

FRIEDRICH NIETZSCHE / Beyond Good and Evil … 49

PART II. WHY MEN FIND IT NATURAL TO DO WHAT IS RIGHT

PLATO / The Virtues in the Individual … 57

JEAN-JACQUES ROUSSEAU / The Natural Man … 62

EARL OF SHAFTESBURY / Virtue and the Natural Affections … 68

JOHN STUART MILL / Utilitarianism … 74

PART III. MORALITY AND HUMAN NATURE

JOHN DEWEY / Does Human Nature Change? … 83

ARISTOTLE / The Good, Virtue, and Friendship and Happiness … 92

IMMANUEL KANT / The Incentive to Morality and Fundamental Law of Pure Practical Reason … 102

JOHN RAWLS / The Sense of Justice … 112

Bibliography … 121

Introduction

It is difficult to say anything about philosophical ethics in general without making it sound more important and exciting than it is. I could say that the task of ethics is to show the grounds of reasonable choice in its relation to happiness; to elucidate the concept of the good life; to investigate ideas like obligation, duty, and responsibility; to decide what ought to be done. Though more or less accurate, such a statement would be misleading. Everyone wants to be happy and would like to be sure that his choices are reasonable; everyone is (at least fitfully) concerned about his duties and obligations; most people worry occasionally about what ought to be done, and some are in a state of perpetual quandary. If solutions to these problems are given by philosophical ethics, then shouldn't we postpone all decisions and drop everything else until we find out what the solutions are? A false hope, alas, doomed to disappointment. A moment's reflection will make the reason evident: acqaintance with philosophical ethics cannot be necessary in order to be wise and happy, since many wise and happy people have never heard of philosophical ethics or, having heard of it, regard it as a trifling, bookish avocation. Nor, on the other hand, does philosophical ethics offer the key to wisdom and happiness; if it did, then philosophers themselves ought to be preeminent in these respects, *much* better off than the rest of us. But this does not seem to be the case, or if it is, it is not as obvious as it ought to be.

One can err, of course, in the other direction: some philosophers, eager to disavow claims to a distinctive practical wisdom or virtue of their own, say that the problems of philosophical ethics are entirely speculative and have no bearing on practical questions about what to do. On the face of it, this view cannot be right either; for one thing, you would have to know more about the relation of theory to practice than anybody does in order to be *sure* that ethics is never of *any* use. Still, if one has to choose, it is probably better to underrate the practical value of ethics: errors will then come as a pleasant surprise rather than as a disappointment.

When one tries to relate ethical theory as a field to the rest of philosophy, there is again the danger of overstatement. Ethics, one could say, is bounded by theory of knowledge, metaphysics, aesthetics, theory of education, and philosophy of law. Surely, then, it must be the heart of philosophy. In a way it is, but this gives it no special honor. One should think, perhaps, of the interior of Australia: maps are fragmentary; much is unexplored; much that has been explored is somewhat arid. But topographical figures of speech are not really apt. For one thing, it is not at all clear that there is a single set of features, a "landscape," which moral philosophers have to describe. It might be better, then, to talk in the plural about ethical *theories,* but in doing so, one must remember that "theory" is a courtesy title. Ethical doctrines are not systems devised for explaining laws or events; they would not be taken by a scientist to be "theories." As a consequence, it may happen that two ethical theories which appear at first to be rivals—in the sense that by accepting one, we preclude acceptance of the other—turn out in the end to be compatible. (Trying to make out the exact point with respect to which two theories actually conflict is a recurrent headache in ethics and in philosophy as a whole.)

I

Another way, perhaps the least misleading, of describing ethics is to say that it consists of assorted sets of more or less coherent comments on a group of related topics such as justice, freedom of the will, reason and the passions, the nature of the good. It is to one such topic that the selections which follow are addressed. Let us give it a title: *Morality and Human Nature.* It sounds discouragingly general and vague, and one could construe it in a way which would make it include all the other topics mentioned. I use it to refer to a particular problem, or group of problems, as will appear.

Since many philosophical puzzles arise from a failure to notice that two philosophers use the same word and yet understand it in different ways, it is important for a critic, a student, an outsider, to be clear about his own assumptions. He must explain what meanings he attaches to terms which are crucial to the discussion. Here a difficulty arises: "morality" and "human nature" are not technical terms: they do not have stipulated meanings that could be looked up in a handbook. But on the other hand they are not quite everyday terms either; most of the time one could get along very well without either of them. They belong really to the vocabulary of reflective generalization and find their proper place in newspaper editorials, commencement addresses, and wise sayings of cracker-barrel philosophers. In their usual contexts, "morality" and "human nature" are extremely vague—not that this matters; those who use them often do not wish or are not able to say anything clear. But serious philosophers do have definite things to say, and when they take over these expressions, they trim and tailor them to meet the requirements of their own particular doctrines. Kant, for example, explains at great length what "morality" means, and Dewey wrote volumes on the concept of "human nature." With so many articulate definitions at hand, we need not confine ourselves to the usage of rhetoricians and journalists. The hitch is that to adopt a philosophical definition is to embrace a theory, that is, to commit oneself to a particular doctrine or point of view. And since, to begin with, we want to *compare* points of view, it seems wrong to prejudge the issue by adopting one in advance. The point at issue here is neither easy nor trivial: in order to make comparisons, we must have a vantage point and yet every genuine vantage point gives us, as it were, a one-sided view.

There are various ways of dealing with this problem. For example, students are sometimes urged to avoid, or at least to postpone, taking any stand themselves so as to appreciate without prejudice the differences between one philosophical position and another. As an illustration, consider the concept of justice: from Plato we learn that justice is the harmony of the soul or the efficient functioning of a community based on division of labor and administered by philosopher-kings. From the contemporary philosopher, John Rawls, we learn that justice is something akin to fair play and is exemplified in a social institution "when it satisfies the principles which those who participate in it could propose to one another for mutual acceptance from an original position of equal liberty."[1] Each of these definitions is expanded and explained in the theories in which they respectively occur. The suggested procedure, then, is that each view should be considered independently and on its own merits, bearing in mind the fact that, for Plato, justice has nothing to do with fair play, and that, for Rawls, justice has nothing to do with efficient administration. The difficulty with this procedure is that it makes the notion of comparing two views very obscure. If, indeed, they differ so radically as to make their common use of the term "justice" seem like an accident, what is the point of comparing

[1] See below p. 115 n. 7.

them? Isn't it like comparing a point of order with a point of no return?

A better procedure, it seems to me, would be as follows: "justice," like "human nature" and "morality," is for most of us a vague term, but not limitlessly vague; it does have a meaning and a use. A proof of this fact is that Rawls' definition, while much more complicated and technical than any impromptu account that we would be likely to give, seems at first appearance to be a plausible extension or refinement of our ordinary notion of justice. Plato's definition, on the other hand, strikes us not exactly as wrong, but rather as peculiar. The reason is that we would ordinarily think that, given a society where things were running smoothly, where everyone was doing just what he was fitted to do and not interfering with anyone else, where philosophers were kings, it would still be perfectly proper—not at all superfluous—to raise the question whether that society satisfied the requirements of justice. If our primary concern were with the history of ideas, we could investigate the influences—Roman law, stoicism, and so forth—which account for our current notion of justice. (Those who are interested in questions of translation might consider whether "justice" is really the proper English word for what Plato had in mind.) Neither project would be possible unless we had a general idea of what we (as it happens) mean when we speak of justice. Before considering what philosophers have had to say about the relation of morality and human nature, I shall try to find, for the two key terms, partial definitions. What is needed is something a little less vague than the original and yet not so precise as to seem unfamiliar or to commit us in advance to a particular philosophical doctrine.

II

For "morality" let us try "the way people ought to behave"—not a great improvement perhaps, but a step in the right direction, away from elevated language and edifying sentiments. Next, let us understand "the way people ought to behave" as comprising elementary rules of right conduct: one should respect other people and treat them fairly; one should help them wherever possible; one should keep one's promises and tell the truth; one should contribute in appropriate ways to the welfare of the community. Given these rules, we can answer the question, "What ought a person to do (in general)?" or "What is the nature of morally right conduct?" Such a question is not often asked seriously—we worry about particular duties rather than about duties in general—but it *can* be asked and now our answer would be a command: "Conduct your life in accord with the following rules." Or we could express each of the rules as a separate command.

If we agree to adopt the preceding explication of "morality," do we thereby avoid the procedural difficulties that I mentioned? Haven't we, in *specifying* the "way people ought to behave," taken a stand and so acquired a bias? The answer is that we have taken a stand, or rather, as it seems to me, acknowledged a commitment, but that we have not adopted a *philosophical* position and thereby disqualified ourselves as philosophical critics. The philosophic differences of opinion which we want to keep straight can be made clear by being set forth in relation to the concept of "morality," as defined above. Suppose, for example, that we were to ask first Plato and then Kant to comment on our version of "the way people ought to behave." Neither would reject it—to do so would be to say of some or all of the rules of right conduct that they might reasonably be ignored, that, for example, it makes no difference morally speaking whether one keeps one's promises and tells the truth or not. At the same time, neither thinker would regard the rules of right conduct as an illuminating answer to the *philosophical* question, "What is the nature of Morality?" Both of them would hold that Morality is something more than what we have agreed here to call "morality." And it is when it comes to setting forth what the relation is between "morality" and Morality that philosophical differences emerge. Their respective positions, stated briefly, are as follows: for Plato the rules of right conduct are taken as indications of how a virtuous man will behave once his intellectual confusions are cleared away and he is able to seek true happiness through the cultivation of his rational faculty. For Kant, the rules of right conduct must be shown to be derived from the Categorical Imperative, a first principle and one that is not itself derived, namely: "So act that thou canst will thy maxim universal law." We can then express the points of difference between Plato and Kant in the following way: for Plato, Morality is essentially a striving for enlightenment and happiness; anyone who actively pursues these goals will observe the rules of right conduct. For Kant, Morality is essentially respect for the moral law as formulated by the Categorical Imperative. Plato and Kant are here taken as examples; subsequently I shall try to show how other philosophical conceptions of Morality can be described in their relation to our notion of "the way people ought to behave."

III

The next step is to decide what we, as critics, are to understand by the expression "human nature" since, as with the concept of morality, we need a vantage point from which to consider philosophic doctrines. Here too, we need something which is less vague than the original expression but which will nonetheless leave open the major questions on which philosophers disagree. It may seem that we are on controversial ground right from the beginning, since to speak of human nature is to commit oneself to the notion that there *is* such a thing. The philosophers represented here would not object, but there are those who take exception. We can bypass this dispute by recognizing the kind of questions on which it turns. One of these is a metaphysical issue: Aristotle believed that things and also persons have essential characteristics which are distinct from accidental characteristics. ("Human nature," according to Aristotle, comprises what is essential to being a man, the characteristics of being a rational animal.) Critics of Aristotle, for reasons into which we do not need to go, object to the distinction, and thus to speaking, in an Aristotelian way, about "human nature." But there is no reason why we cannot use the expression to refer to characteristics which are common and peculiar to human beings without regard to the merits of the alleged distinction between those which are essential and those which are accidental.

Some existentialists reject the notion of human nature on moral grounds: Sartre, for example, thinks that believing in a fixed pattern, a kind of model human being, has bad psychological effects since it leads people to forget that each of us is an individual and individually responsible for what he becomes. Sartre may be right in fact, although at face value his point seems rather farfetched. In any event, there is no logical reason why a person should not understand that he is similar to other people in some respects and not in others and that, where moral decisions have to be made, individual differences should be taken into account.

We can talk about human nature, then, without bringing in essences or models and without suggesting that differences don't count. But we have to place some limit on the characteristics which we are to include; human beings have, for example, anatomical characteristics which distinguish them, although perhaps not very sharply, from other species. These are taken for granted when one talks about human nature. What about physiologically determined needs, instincts, and drives? These are borderline cases: Dewey includes them as part of "human nature" and indeed suggests that they may be the *only* characteristics which are genuinely invariant. Consider next psychological features such as motives and goals; they seem to be the center of attention for most philosophers who talk of human nature. Here again we must dodge a controversy: our first thought is that while it may be peculiar to human beings that they *have* motives and goals, it is silly to imagine that they all have the *same* motives and goals. On the contrary, it seems obvious that variety is ultimate; men are moved to act by ambition, generosity, patriotism, fear, and the like. As to goals, according to one way of looking at the matter, there are as many goals as there are individuals striving to achieve something. There are philosophers and also psychologists who, without denying the obvious facts, believe that a deeper analysis of human behavior supports the hypothesis that there is some single dominant motive, such as the will to power, which underlies the multiplicity of human endeavors. Or they argue that the variety of goals which people profess, such as finding a job, or winning a race are, if properly understood, intermediate stages in the pursuit of one final goal, such as happiness or ego-gratification. These theorists explain "human nature" by referring to their respective views about what the "real" as distinguished from the professed reasons are for human conduct. The situation parallels the one I noted in the case of "morality": ordinary rules of right conduct which delimit the way people ought to behave are a mixed lot. That one should help those who need help and that one should tell the truth are two requirements that seem just to *be* two. But as I showed, taking Plato and Kant as examples, there are philosophers who believe that this apparent heterogeneity ought not to be taken at face value, and that apparently unrelated rules of conduct are really special applications of one fundamental rule or imperative or strategy, and that unless one understands this, one may be familiar with "morality," but have failed to grasp Morality.

My proposal is that, in order to compare philosophical doctrines about Human Nature and Morality, we take as a starting point human nature at face value in its multiform and variable aspects. Morality is to be understood as the rules of right conduct, the familiar precepts which embody our idea of the way people ought to behave. We are on safe ground in that philosophers, while they may transcend or systematize these vague common-sense ideas, cannot afford to ignore them. One further question, again controversial, but one which nonetheless must be answered tentatively, is how we think we get to know what human nature is and, further, how we know what the rules of right conduct are. As to the former, we pay attention to the way people act, beginning with ourselves, our friends and associates, and then consider what we learn from the press and from professional observers such as historians and sociologists. The rules of right conduct we learn originally from our parents or other authorities and then, when we get to the stage of recognizing that parents and authorities are not infallible, by deciding for ourselves what rules of conduct we really ought to observe.

IV

Suppose now that we consider the relation between morality and human nature as we, for the time being, understand them. One question is, given the rules of right conduct, what can be said about the way that people actually behave? The proper way to answer is to begin by considering those one knows and then, since this group, even for the most sociable, is rather small, one can go on to include those whose actions we learn about indirectly. A study of history or anthropology widens our horizons and helps diminish provincialism by making it less likely that we shall mistake a local tendency to be a trait that is universally shared. There is room for differences of opinion, but no one, I suppose, denies that there is a striking discrepancy between actual human conduct and conduct that is morally right. One's impression is that on the whole we are less than truthful, often unkind, preoccupied with private projects, and only fitfully concerned with the interests and rights of others.

Moreover, this impression is reinforced by a consideration of human history. Morally speaking, it is at best an undistinguished record—according to Voltaire, "a record of crimes against humanity." Of course, there are exceptions: we come across individuals, groups, even official groups or institutions, that preserve standards of charity and justice under stress. These exceptions are important, no matter how rare; if some people are not a total loss then it is reasonable to suppose that not everyone *has* to be. Such cases constitute a challenge for philosophers who hold that human nature is inherently corrupt. Conversely, of course, philosophers who claim to discover in all men a natural affinity with the right and the good have to show that in arriving at this conclusion, they have considered human conduct in the main and not just exceptional cases, saints and heroes.

That human beings frequently do not behave the way they ought is not a novel or interesting observation. Nonethless, it is true and, given the interpretations of morality and human nature which we have adopted here, plus the requirement that something be said about the relation of the two in *general,* it is perhaps all that can be said. (If, instead of looking for a general answer, we were to examine or construct concrete cases, as literary artists do, then the results could be novel and interesting.) It seems likely that questions suggested by my truism are among the incentives which lead philosophers to construct general theories. For example, one may wonder in a practical way whether, in the light of past performance, there is any point in trying to institute moral reforms. If the answer is yes, then there is the question of how to proceed: what methods are appropriate to moral education? If the answer is no, then should not one consider whether there is something wrong with the requirements of morality itself? (On analogy, one might say that an examination which nobody—or almost nobody— had a hope of passing was a defective examination, and did not serve its purpose.)

V

I noted above that a concept of human nature is derived from observations and records of human behavior. It might be argued that anyone who is seriously interested in the question—serious enough to want to go beyond the level of casual impressions— ought to turn to the psychologists rather than to the philosophers. One could also argue that in a genuine theory of human nature there is no place for censorious comments on human conduct or for other evaluative judgments. Morality, it has been said, belongs to the "realm of values," concern for which is proper to philosophers, theologians, and artists. But a theory of human nature is part of science and belongs to the "realm of fact." This line of argument must be considered briefly since the philosophers represented in the following selections find frequent occasion to make evaluative judgments: Aristotle extols the pleasures of contemplation; Kant warns against the dangers of equating righteousness with benevolence; Nietzsche derides the cult of sympathy. These examples might be adduced in support of the claim that the *philosophical* issue of Morality and Human Nature belongs entirely to the "realm of value," and that it is a mistake to speak of *contrasting* Morality and Human Nature, when the latter is explained in language borrowed from the former.

It must be admitted that a good deal of what philosophers have to say about human nature sounds more like a character reference than an essay in psychology. In this respect, philosophical psychology, if I may so describe it, resembles everyday conversation, which, apart from shoptalk, consists largely of gossip. In expressing one's views of a person's character, that is, of those habits, abilities, and capacities which seem relatively stable, it is natural to use words such as *ambitious, generous, vain,* and so forth. In many contexts such expressions convey approval or disapproval, praise or blame, and so one would expect, since our interest in one another's character is largely practical, that is, bound up with questions about how to get along together. One can convey praise or blame not only by attributing traits of character to a particular person but also by ascribing to him a particular act which falls within the range of one of the rules of right conduct. Thus, to say of someone that he betrayed a secret, broke a promise, or relieved human suffering is to say *what* he did and in the same breath, as it were, to award merits or demerits to him for doing it.

If our primary interest is in *explaining* human conduct, by finding psychological laws which can be tested experimentally, then it is convenient to revise our ordinary vocabulary in such a way as to minimize critical and moralizing overtones. Instead of saying that someone is bad-tempered or irritable, we say that he has a low frustration-tolerance; instead of saying that he is clever, we say that he has a high IQ. Such technical terms are not just neutral replacements for everyday terms; the difference between statements about someone's cleverness and about his IQ are more than stylistic or rhetorical. In psychology, as in other sciences, it may be necessary to create a vocabulary in order to be able to discuss things or characteristics for which everyday language contains no words. Again, where new techniques of measurement or testing are introduced, then even if the results can be described informally, it is sometimes better to use a technical term.[2]

Of course, even without inventing technical terms we can try to describe a person's conduct and refrain from comments or criticisms; witnesses in court are called upon to do so. Historians and journalists are supposed to cultivate the ability to record actions and events without making moral judgments or evaluations. It requires skill and practice because this way of speaking is slightly abnormal. Success is a matter of degree; two newspaper accounts, for example, may be distinguished on the basis of the degree of editorializing they exhibit. It does not follow that there is some ideal of neutral reportage to which every chronicler aspires. Whether such an ideal is even possible is a question on which philosophers disagree.

Of the authors whose views on human nature are set forth in the following selections none is concerned with *experimental* psychology, with laboratory techniques or statistical procedures. In that respect one could say that they are "unscientific," but so, of course, is a large part of what is included in academic psychology. Further, all of them are concerned with the specifically moral capacities of human beings and in that sense with human values. In the extent to which by characterizing human nature philosophers convey their own favorable or unfavorable comments, there is, as one would expect, a wide range of difference. Aristotle, Dewey, Rawls, and Mill set forth their views in an idiom which is relatively neutral and just in that sense "scientific"; Rousseau, Plato, and Shaftesbury are less constrained and do not find it inappropriate to apostrophize what they approve and condemn what they find evil. There is no obvious reason for preferring one manner to the other.

Despite the difficulty in finding any single determinate criterion

[2] The exact nature of the relation between such technical terms and their informal counterparts is difficult to state and probably varies from case to case. Under some conditions but not under others, it would be silly to say: "He may have a high IQ but he's not very bright." The general question about uses of language and how one use is connected with another is quite technical and I shall not try to discuss it here. One thing that may be noticed is that technical terms often come to be everyday terms and then may acquire evaluative force. (The word *neurotic* is a case in point.)

for distinguishing "values" from "facts," many people are convinced that the difference is crucial. One reason may be that what they have in mind is the difference, which *is* crucial, between fair and objective accounts as opposed to those which are the product of prejudice and bias. This distinction (also a matter of degree) is independent of subject matter and cuts across the difference between describing or explaining, on the one hand, and evaluating, on the other. Impartiality, like honesty, is a universal requirement for anyone who claims authority for his opinions. Physicists, no less than historians or psychologists, are expected to guard against wishful thinking and the distortion of evidence by personal likes and dislikes. Being impartial requires practice, but, unlike being noncommittal, it is not a stylistic skill and does not consist in avoiding criticism or evaluation. The aim is rather that evaluation should be reasonable and fair. Confusion is possible on this point because of the unfortunate word *objective*, which is sometimes taken to mean noncommittal and sometimes to mean "equitable" or "impartial." There really is no connection: testimony which is "factual," that is, relatively nonevaluative, may still be biased, and explicit evaluations may be reasonable and just.

To say that a moral philosopher is not impartial is a serious criticism, and one that should not be made without detailed support. As a possible example, consider Nietzsche's remarks to the effect that utilitarianism is insular and imbued with the spirit of moral hypocrisy. In application to Mill, at least, the objections seem spiteful and unfair.

VI

The question may arise whether a philosopher can present an account of true Morality which by implication or directly would invalidate the ordinary rules of right conduct which we take to define morality. At first appearance the views of Nietzsche or of Plato's Thrasymachus seem to be examples: both depend on the notion that exceptional individuals are exempt from ordinary moral rules and that only the untalented and timid majority need concern itself with paying debts, helping those in distress, and keeping promises. It is difficult to tell what this doctrine in its various versions would amount to, in practice. According to Thrasymachus, it appears that the exceptional individual is not bound by any rules; he is perpetually free to do whatever he likes. Nietzsche, on the other hand, appears to envisage a special "higher morality" for the superior individuals, and the issue is complicated by the fact that with respect to certain rules, for instance truth-telling, the "higher morality" seems to coincide with the ordinary rules meant for inferior people. Some of the puzzles involved in this view may be postponed for later discussion. Here we may note that neither Thrasymachus nor Nietzsche denies the *utility* of morality, given the abilities of the ignoble majority, and neither seems to look forward to the day when *everyone* will be exceptional. What these points suggest is that the "higher morality" for the superior few may be in some sense dependent on the concept of ordinary morality.

Something which approaches closer to a rejection of morality appears in some doctrines described as "crisis" philosophies. Rather than making a few superior people exempt from ordinary moral rules, "crisis" philosophies hold that everyone is exempt because of very special circumstances, for example, the imminence of some large-scale catastrophe such as The Day of Judgment. These doctrines are easier to understand than to defend. One can see how people in a state of panic may forget everything they ever learned, including the ordinary rules of right conduct; yet, although such behavior might be condoned, one cannot imagine how it could reasonably be recommended. In fact, as we shall see, exponents of "crisis" philosophy do not repudiate *all* rules of conduct; they generally advocate some spiritual *stance* such as courage in the face of the Absurd (Camus) or submission to the will of God. In contrast with Plato and Kant, who take Morality to be something more than ordinary rules of right conduct, the crisis philosophers take Morality to be something less than those rules.

VII

As I suggested earlier, the proper way to compare one philosopher's concept of Morality with another is to see how each of them is related to the rules of right conduct which make explicit our concept of morality, or the way people ought to behave. It is tempting to think that one can argue for the merits of this procedure by showing that acceptance of morality, in the ordinary sense, is a common factor, a point on which philosophers agree. I am not sure whether or not this claim can be established; certainly it cannot be established directly. For example, if what it takes to prove agreement is an explicit avowal ("I agree that one should tell the truth, keep one's promises . . . ," signed "Plato," "Kant," and so on), then it cannot be done. But perhaps that requirement is too strong: we do not always make people recite credos before deciding what it is they believe. In ordinary cases, if we notice that a person does habitually treat others with respect, tell the truth, and so forth, we conclude that he accepts the rules of right conduct. But now at the moment we are not interested in the *moral character* of any individual philosopher but rather in his doctrine, and that brings us back again to what he says or writes, and hence (apparently) to a dead end.

The only possibility would be to argue for each individual philosopher that what he does say implies or presupposes that he accepts ordinary rules of right conduct. But unless one had a clear account of how to tell what implies what—which is not a simple matter—then this would be a dubious line of argument. One obvious fact is that if you select philosophers from one cultural tradition, broadly speaking, then it will not be surprising if they turn out to concur on what constitutes the rules of right conduct. Perhaps if I had included some Kwakiutls, things would look different. But then again perhaps not: there is a certain intuitive force in the notion that any group, if it is to be stable enough to produce theories about morality, must acknowledge social obligations of some sort. Furthermore, although you would expect local differences—for instance, there is no point in having a rule about yam-planting where there are no yams—it is hard to imagine any socially workable set of rules which did not include or assume the obligation to keep promises, help those in distress, and so forth. This is a topic for speculation and I shall not pursue it further.

Returning to the question of alternative philosophical accounts of morality: once their differences have been made clear, how does one decide on their relative merits? Certain requirements we can be sure of, since they hold for any theory: consistency is such a requirement and beyond consistency, "coherence," a feature which it is easier to appreciate than to define. But what about specific criteria for theories of Morality? At least the following seems appropriate: whatever the essential nature of the Good is discovered to be, it must not be radically unattainable: whatever is proposed as the foundation of the Right or the basic Moral Law must not be such that nobody can ever do what is right. Some qualifications are needed: for Plato, the Form Of The Good, which is the source of value, is located (or rather non-located) in a spaceless eternal realm of essence and so it *is* radically unattainable. But Plato does have some arguments designed to show that the Good, remote though it is, can and does function as a goal and a source of illumination for human striving. His arguments do not look very persuasive, but still they ought to be taken seriously. Kant, to take another example, says (in *Foundations of the Metaphysics of Morals*) that a person can know for sure that he has failed to do his duty, failed, that is, to act out of respect for the Moral Law, but that he can never be sure that he has *done* his duty. This discouraging conclusion need not perhaps be accepted. Kant's argument—that it is impossible to be sure of one's own incentives and motives—cuts both ways. One's sense of moral failure is not an infallible sign of moral failure. To make his point plausible, Kant would have to explain how it is that introspective insight is reliable only where what it discovers is a non-moral or selfish reason for action.

In any event, the criterion of what might be called "feasibility" is not intended to exclude out of hand any of the theories presented here. What the criterion does, though, is remind us of why it is important to have an adequate notion of human nature. In extreme cases it is clear enough. Aristotle, for example, believes that happiness, the goal of the good life, consists in "rational activity in accord with virtue." And virtue is said to involve an inner discipline with respect to habits of choice; in any situation where alternatives are available, one must decide by reflection what action would be appropriate, the mean between excess and defect. But if the account of human nature which is illustrated in the Myth of Gyges is credible, then happiness, as Aristotle understands it, is an impossible goal. For a population whose appetites and aggressive impulses are kept in check only by immediate direct threats of retaliation or punishment, Aristotelian Morality would make no sense. In other words, if the Gyges-view of human nature is true, then Aristotle's theory can be ruled out by reference to the criterion of feasibility.

VIII

For reasons mentioned in section I, attempted classification of ethical theories yields depressing results. Ideas which are actually quite interesting can come to seem pointless and dull as the result of clumsy paraphrase. (That is one reason for starting with selections such as those in this book.) On the other hand, having read the works of philosophers themselves, it is sometimes helpful to see how far one can get in an attempt to order their respective views in the light of a single question.

As an example of the kind of experiment I have in mind, consider the following: Assume that what is central is a practical, in particular, a pedagogical, problem. The moral philosopher who claims special authority—although not necessarily special privilege—is a teacher, and his instruction is designed to advance the moral education of mankind at large. He begins, let us say, with a general idea of what he wants to achieve but is prepared to be flexible within certain limits and to revise the curriculum in the light of information about the needs and capacities of the students. What he has to teach are the rules of right conduct, and his most immediate aim is to induce students to observe these rules, that is, to act in acccord with the injunctions about telling the truth, not injuring others, and so forth. (Here is one point where the hypothesis becomes artificial: the first stage of moral education is carried out not by philosophers but by parents and other authorities. But unless it *were* carried out, the philosopher-teacher could not get on to the further stages, and so it does no harm to include it.) Besides learning to observe the rules of right conduct, it is desirable that the student should come to see what the point of those rules is; that is the second part of the project.

Getting through the first step, that is, learning to observe the rules, is a task which makes rather heavy demands on the student. First of all, it requires intelligence: he must be bright enough to recognize occasions on which the rules apply. (Notice that even the simplest examples of, say, promise-keeping are fairly complex.) And he must be capable of calculating, at least for the short run, consequences of his own and other people's actions. Second, he must have a measure of self-control, because following a rule, that is, acting on principle, is sometimes disagreeable. Third, he must be autonomous, at least to the extent of being able to go on putting his lessons to use in the absence of supervision and advice. And this last requirement means that he must be capable of wanting or resolving to follow the rules, although he need not have a very clear idea why.

Suppose now that the instructor came to believe that all of his students were unalterably defective in one or other of these respects. He might conclude, taking the Myth of Gyges at face value, that they are just unable to control themselves where physical restraints are absent. He might, were he persuaded of the truth of Calvinism, come to believe that inasmuch as their nature is "totally vicious and depraved" there is no hope of inducing them to want to act according to the rules of right conduct. What would be the sensible thing to do? The instructor, one might say, ought to resign. In fact, however, Calvin and those who share his views manage to make out that men can, by the help of Divine Grace, learn how to act in accord with moral principles, even though they lack part of what is essential in doing so. This sounds on the face of it like a contradiction, and I believe that further analysis shows that it *is* a contradiction. Complicated theological questions make it difficult, however, to be sure of what Calvin means. It is interesting to note that in specifying what man's duty or vocation actually is, the main emphasis is on submission to temporal power. Philosophers, Calvin remarks, often encourage the killing of tyrants as a praiseworthy deed, but such an act would always be condemned by the "Celestial Judge." It does seem plausible that one who holds that moral education (at least as I have defined it) is impossible, and who nonetheless is unwilling to abdicate the role of preceptor, should think of advising his students to conform to existing institutional practices and to eschew rebellion.

Suppose, to consider a further possibility, that you come to believe that Calvinism is not, as it appears to be, incoherent, and that it is actually true. Moral values, indeed *all* values, will appear to depend on the will of God. And then suppose you are led to the conclusion that believing in God is a mistake, and that no such omnipotent being or Celestial Judge exists. This, I take it, is something like the position from which Camus begins: since God does not exist, the universe lacks meaning and is thus, in relation to man, "absurd." In a famous essay, Sartre expresses the point in the following way:

> The existentialist . . . thinks it very distressing that God does not exist, because all possibility of finding values in a heaven of ideas disappears along with Him. . . . Nowhere is it written that the Good exists, that we must be honest, that we must not lie; because the fact is we are on a plane where there are only men. Dostoievsky said, 'If God didn't exist, everything would be possible'. That is the very starting point of existentialism.
>
> *Existentialism* (tr. Frechtman)

At the beginning of the Myth of Sisyphus (a section not included in this book), Camus says that "the only truly serious philosophical problem is suicide," the question, that is, whether in the face of "absurdity" it would not be appropriate to kill oneself. If Camus genuinely believed that this is the *only* problem, then I suppose one could say that he really had resigned, or refrained from applying for, the office of moral teacher. And yet he, and Sartre too, manage to extract from their initial premise a number of bits of advice about how to behave in a meaningless world. Camus makes two points in particular: first, one should refrain from suicide. Facing the absurd requires courage, rather like living with a fatal disease, and in doing this, one should be guided by the thought that "what counts is not the best of living but the most living." As far as this notion is explained, it sounds like the search for pleasure or happiness and if this is correct then Camus, after all, is in agreement with Mill, Aristotle, and many other traditional philosophers, who also, of course, find room for the virtue of courage. The question remains whether these two rules, even if one learned to obey them, are sufficient to count as a moral education. It seems to me that they are not. Moreover, unless one can sympathize with the extremely peculiar notion that God's nonexistence somehow blurs the distinction between right and wrong, the existentialist lesson will seem not only meager but pointless.

IX

Next we may imagine that our hypothetical moral teacher progresses to the stage of realizing that whether life is absurd or not, most people value it and will go to a certain amount of trouble to preserve it. He also comes to think that the greatest threat to life is universal war and that the onset of such a war is a perpetual danger in view of the deep-rooted human desire for power and self-aggrandizement. Now he has become something of a Hobbesian. Given his views of human capacity, moral education, or at any rate the first step, becomes possible. Although his putative students are so constituted as to find acting on principle uncongenial, they are able to control their aggressions and are intelligent enough to see that the only alternative to respect for principle is general disaster. To be sure, one must suppose a sovereign in the background who has enough power to keep the peace. As long as he can retain it, his power confers authority and a measure of privilege, but no particular sanctity or virtue. (Here it is interesting to consider Hobbes's views on the authority of God.) Revolutions are to be avoided since they are likely to bring about regression to the "state of nature," in which everyone is bound to be nervous and miserable. On the other hand, since it is more important to have *some* authority than to have one rather than another, a revolution which seems assured of success is justified.

Hobbes is one of those philosophers who cultivate a spirit of moral detachment. His account of human nature suggests an agreement with Calvinism but he eschews terms such as "envy," "concupiscence," and "depravity" in favor of a more neutral vocabulary. In contrast to the Platonic Callicles and to Nietzsche, Hobbes is unmoved by thoughts of the inherent dignity of power, and what distinguishes his view from theirs is more than a difference of temperament. A moral educator who believes in the utility of rules of right conduct but also finds something to admire in the individual who acts in violation of those rules or, as such philosophers say, "transcends" them, is in an awkward pedagogical position. Indeed it might seem impossible to inculcate observance of principles while at the same time encouraging particular individuals to repudiate them. The solution is to divide the class, so to speak, into two groups, gifted students and dull normals. Nietzsche seems to have believed that utilitarianism and Christian doctrine, both of which foster a regard for ordinary rules of right conduct, are not only appropriate but necessary for the dull-witted majority. He also predicted (as it turned out, incorrectly) the advent of a race of "noble spirits" to the historical scene and proclaimed the need for a "higher morality" or an "anti-morality" which would provide a focus for their superior talents.

It is difficult to conjecture exactly what might go on in the advanced class; at times it would seem as though the main occupation were to be making fun of the dull normals, an occupation which strikes one as both unworthy of a "noble spirit" and somewhat tedious. (For Callicles' strong man, this problem does not arise: he is excused from school altogether and may do just as he pleases.) The fundamental question which exponents of both views leave unanswered (I am not sure whether or not it arises in the case of Hobbes) is why—that is, what shadow of reason there could be for anyone to think—superiority of intellect, imagination, or what not is grounds for claiming exemption from the rules of right conduct. The oddity of the whole idea comes out if we think of concrete cases: someone who is shown to have broken a promise or betrayed a friend offers as his defence evidence of unusual intelligence. His claim is not even a poor excuse; it is a simple non sequitur.

To be fair to Nietzsche, it must be admitted that sometimes he conveys the impression that the "noble spirits" are to be free, not in being exempt from ordinary rules, but rather in being emancipated from petty concerns, hypocrisy, and pharisaism. If one reads him this way, then Nietzsche ought not to be compared with Hobbes or Bentham and Mill, all of whom thought in terms of a program which could actually be put into effect. Instead, Nietzsche belongs with Shaw and Ibsen: his target is not morality as such but, rather, the moral deficiencies of contemporary social conventions.

X

Figurative devices ought not to be elaborated to the point of tediousness and perhaps it is time to forget our hypothetical moral instructor. Anyone who finds it useful to continue the story will find it easy to do so. Shaftesbury, Rousseau, and Dewey will appear in opposition to Hobbes, each of them finding in his observation of human nature reason to believe that morality is not a painful yoke but rather an ordering of benevolent impulse and hence a means of self-fulfillment.

The doctrine of Kant will require separate consideration because of the peculiar importance ascribed to what I called the second stage of moral education, namely the explication of the grounds of morality. Kant's claim is partly negative in the following sense: he believes that of all the previously mentioned reasons for acting according to the rules of right conduct—as, for example, that it is in the long run less inconvenient to do so, or that doing so fulfills fundamental human desires—none is really a *sufficient* reason. By "sufficient reason" he seems to mean two things which are not always easy to distinguish: first, he suggests that people who are induced to do what they ought to do by the belief that they will be better off or happier, will never actually achieve autonomy, the capacity to apply rules to novel situations and in the absence of immediate constraint; and autonomy, as noted, is one of the requirements of moral education. For example, "honesty is the best policy" may be true, but Kant's claim is that anyone who is honest *only* out of considerations of policy is unlikely to be consistently honest. Here, one would think, the question at issue is open to speculation: if honesty really *is* the best policy, and if human beings are sufficiently intelligent to recognize, given suitable instruction, a good policy when they see one, then it seems possible that they *could* learn to be consistently and unexceptionably honest. But even if they did, this would not satisfy Kant because, by "sufficient reason," he also means something other than "causally efficacious incentive." As reasons for being honest, considerations of policy are *morally* insufficient, and so are all other considerations, except one, namely, a sense of duty or regard for the Moral Law. Like Hobbes, Kant is impressed by the need for strongly reinforced constraint of natural inclinations, all of which he regards as inherently self-interested and antisocial. Constraint is exercised by the inner authority of conscience, which recognizes the Moral Law as supreme and imposes its mandates, as Kant says, "unconditionally," that is, without regard for particular circumstances or for the wishes or desires of the moral agent. (The Kantian idiom, in which psychological features are personified—I listen to the "voice of conscience" as it issues "commands" which my passions "obey"—is extremely confusing. It is never clear how many speaking parts there are in the moral drama. A similar muddle results from Plato's insistence on describing the "soul" as a little bureaucracy.)

Every individual, according to Kant, must "legislate for himself"; he must assume, with respect to his own conduct, the role which the Hobbesian sovereign has with respect to the surly citizenry. The autonomy thereby achieved is not anarchistic though, since in legislating for himself each individual also legislates for every rational being.

Kantian doctrine is difficult and in summary it sounds more obscure than (perhaps) it is. Sometimes, Kant's main point seems clear and obviously right: if you are going to act on the principle, say, of telling the truth, then you must *act on that principle* and not as impulse moves you or as expedience directs. Of course, Mill could agree with that, and so, in a way, could Hobbes. The difference is that, for Hobbes and Mill, it is conceivable that a change of circumstance—though it would have to be a radical one—would justify the revision or emendation of some of the rules of right conduct, whereas according to Kant such a move would always be evidence of moral laxity. Any *kind* of act, such as telling a lie, which is morally wrong must always and under every conceivable set of circumstances be wrong. In the absence of a clear account of what is meant by "telling a lie," Kant's claim is puzzling. If to tell a lie is to utter a falsehood, then Kant seems to be in error, since one can imagine circumstances in which one *would* be morally justified in lying. On the other hand, if to tell a lie is to utter a *culpable* falsehood, then Kant's claim is redundant. This ambiguity affects a number of Kant's fundamental theses. Nonetheless, what he says is interesting: in characterizing the basic moral attitude as one of "respect," he is closer to the truth than those who give first place to benevolence or to prudence. His idea of the fundamental moral principle, expressed as one version of the Categorical Imperative—that one should treat other people as ends and not merely as means—seems intuitively correct, although it is far from easy to explain.

CONCLUSION

Philosophical doctrines of Morality are not designed to *replace* the rules of right conduct, but rather to show their significance by relating them to a broader theoretical context. Generalization about goals is hazardous, but most moral philosophers have tried to simplify, by one means or another, the task of the person who wants to know what it would be right to do. Why should "simplification" be called for? One answer might be that in actual practice (which differs in this respect from my artificial hypothesis) we learn the rules of right conduct in the course of learning a lot of other rules and acquiring habits, tastes and preferences. By reflecting on what we have learned, we may be able to abstract those principles which we take to have the widest generality and the highest authority. But what emerges is likely to be rather scrappy and haphazard in appearance. For some people, such a result is intellectually unsatisfactory and so they are led to look for unifying principles.

Another question which seems to call for a theoretical solution is how one distinguishes a moral rule from a technical rule or a rule of polite social behavior. If one were persuaded that all—and only—moral rules bear a distinctive relation to "The Good" (Plato) or to the "greatest happiness of the greatest number" (Mill), then it would be easier to sort them out. A conscientious person would take on the discrimination of rules as "moral" to be an essential part in deliberating about what he ought to do. But a non-conscientious person, even one who was resolved to be wicked, might feel some curiosity about the criteria for a rule's being a moral one (with a view perhaps to assuring himself that he was being genuinely wicked and not merely unconventional). It is to such questions and interests, practical and theoretical, that the doctrines of moral philosophers are addressed.

When it comes to deciding which, if any, of the philosophical doctrines to accept, then questions about human nature come to the fore. Some philosophers see Morality as being (like the Sabbath) made for man; others think the opposite. Either view, if it is taken seriously, requires assumptions about what people in general *can* do and also about what, under various conditions, they are *likely* to do. To make explicit and to defend one rather than another set of assumptions is to put forward a theory of human nature. How is the adequacy of such theories to be tested? No general answer is possible, because theories diverge not only as to what they assert but in the nature of the evidence or the arguments which they bring to the support of their assertions. So, for example, it is conceivable that Shaftesbury's hypothesis—all who are malicious and selfish are miserable—could be shown by statistical means to be false, or perhaps true under some conditions but not under others. By contrast, no amount of statistical research would suffice to discredit the Calvinist view of human nature or, for that matter, the Kantian view. The claims of the former rest on a basis of scriptural authority and those of the latter on introspective self-examination. There are difficult cases—Hobbes and Aristotle are examples—where one is not sure just where experiment and observation might be relevant and where they would not. The proper procedure then would be to take up each theory separately and to test those substantive claims which are capable of being tested by whatever means is appropriate. Such a project, if it can be carried out, may yield results useful in determining the merits of the various philosophical doctrines of Morality.

PART I
Why Men Find It Hard to Do What Is Right

PLATO

The Myth of Gyges [1]

Born in 427/8 B.C. *to one of Athens' most distinguished families, Plato was greatly influenced by his teacher Socrates, who appears as the major figure in Plato's philosophical dialogues, such as* Euthyphro, Apology, Crito, Phaedo, The Republic, Protagoras, Gorgias, *and* Philebus. *The manner of Socrates' death turned his pupil away from politics and committed him to the less chaotic life of a philosopher-teacher. Plato established the first of the great schools of ancient Greece, the Academy in Athens. When he was past sixty, Plato was offered a chance to test his ideal of the philosopher-king; he was called upon to teach Dionysius II of Syracuse. The experiment was unsuccessful and Plato thereafter confined his attention to teaching and writing. He died in 347/8* B.C.

What people say is that to do wrong is, in itself, a desirable thing; on the other hand, it is not at all desirable to suffer wrong, and the harm to the sufferer outweighs the advantage to the doer. Consequently, when men have had a taste of both, those who have

From *The Republic of Plato,* trans. F. M. Cornford (Oxford: Clarendon Press, 1951), Bk. II, pp. 43–45. Used by permission of the Clarendon Press, Oxford.

[1] *The Republic* is a dialogue in which Socrates defends the thesis that justice, rather than injustice, leads to happiness and argues for the Platonic conception of justice as harmonious functioning of the parts of the soul or, on the political level, the classes in the state. The Sophist position is that it is injustice that leads to happiness, at least for anyone clever enough to avoid punishment. In Book II Glaucon sets forth the basic arguments for the Sophist's doctrine, intending them as a challenge to Socrates.—Ed.

not the power to seize the advantage and escape the harm decide that they would be better off if they made a compact neither to do wrong nor to suffer it. Hence they began to make laws and covenants with one another; and whatever the law prescribed they called lawful and right. That is what right or justice is and how it came into existence; it stands half-way between the best thing of all—to do wrong with impunity—and the worst, which is to suffer wrong without the power to retaliate. So justice is accepted as a compromise, and valued, not as good in itself, but for lack of power to do wrong; no man worthy of the name, who had that power, would ever enter into such a compact with anyone; he would be mad if he did. That, Socrates, is the nature of justice according to this account, and such the circumstances in which it arose.

The next point is that men practise it against the grain, for lack of power to do wrong. How true that is, we shall best see if we imagine two men, one just, the other unjust, given full licence to do whatever they like, and then follow them to observe where each will be led by his desires. We shall catch the just man taking the same road as the unjust; he will be moved by self-interest, the end which it is natural to every creature to pursue as good, until forcibly turned aside by law and custom to respect the principle of equality.

Now, the easiest way to give them that complete liberty of action would be to imagine them possessed of the talisman found by Gyges, the ancestor of the famous Lydian. The story tells how he was a shepherd in the King's service. One day there was a great storm, and the ground where his flock was feeding was rent by an earthquake. Astonished at the sight, he went down into the chasm and saw, among other wonders of which the story tells, a brazen horse, hollow, with windows in its sides. Peering in, he saw a dead body, which seemed to be of more than human size. It was naked save for a gold ring, which he took from the finger and made his way out. When the shepherds met, as they did every month, to send an account to the King of the state of his flocks, Gyges came wearing the ring. As he was sitting with the others, he happened to turn the bezel of the ring inside his hand. At once he became invisible, and his companions, to his surprise, began to speak of him as if he had left them. Then, as he was fingering the ring, he turned the bezel outwards and became visible again. With that, he set about testing the ring to see if it really had this power, and always with the same result: according as he turned the bezel inside or out he vanished and reappeared. After this discovery he contrived to be one of the messengers sent to the court. There he seduced the Queen, and with her help murdered the King and seized the throne.

Now suppose there were two such magic rings, and one were given to the just man, the other to the unjust. No one, it is commonly believed, would have such iron strength of mind as to stand fast in doing right or keep his hands off other men's goods, when he could go to the market-place and fearlessly help himself to anything he wanted, enter houses and sleep with any woman he chose, set prisoners free and kill men at his pleasure, and in a word go about among men with the powers of a god. He would behave no better than the other; both would take the same course. Surely this would be strong proof that men do right only under compulsion; no individual thinks of it as good for him personally, since he does wrong whenever he finds he has the power. Every man believes that wrongdoing pays him personally much better, and, according to this theory, that is the truth. Granted full licence to do as he liked, people would think him a miserable fool if they found him refusing to wrong his neighbours or to touch their belongings, though in public they would keep up a pretence of praising his conduct, for fear of being wrong themselves. So much for that.

Natural Justice

[Callicles, a Sophist, speaks]

By nature, in fact, everything that is worse is uglier, just as suffering wrong is; but to do wrong is uglier merely by convention. For to suffer wrong is not the part of a man at all, but that of a slave for whom it is better to be dead than alive, as it is for anyone who is unable to come either to his own assistance when he is wronged or mistreated or to that of anyone he cares about. I can quite imagine that the manufacturers of laws and conventions are the weak, the majority, in fact. It is for themselves and their own advantage that they make their laws and distribute their

From *Plato's Gorgias*, trans. W. C. Helmbold, copyright, 1952, by The Liberal Arts Press, Inc., p. 51-52, and reprinted by permission of The Liberal Arts Press Division of The Bobbs-Merrill Company, Inc.

praises and their censures. It is to frighten men who are stronger than they and able to enforce superiority that they keep declaring, to prevent aggrandizement, that this is ugly and unjust, that injustice consists in seeking to get the better of one's neighbor. They are quite content, I suppose, to be on equal terms with others since they are themselves inferior.

This, then, is the reason why convention declares that it is unjust and ugly to seek to get the better of the majority. But my opinion is that nature herself reveals it to be only just and proper that the better man should lord it over his inferior: it will be the stronger over the weaker. Nature, further, makes it quite clear in a great many instances that this is the true state of affairs, not only in the other animals, but also in whole states and communities. This is, in fact, how justice is determined: the stronger shall rule and have the advantage over his inferior. By what principle of justice, then, did Xerxes invade Greece or his father Scythia? One could, of course, cite innumerable examples of the same sort of thing. To my mind men are acting in accordance with natural justice when they perform such acts, and, by heaven, it is in accordance with law, too, the law of nature—though, no doubt, it hardly coincides with the one we frame when we mold the natures of the best and strongest among us, raising them from infancy by the incantations of a charmed voice, as men do lion cubs; we enslave them by repeating again and again that equality is morality and only this is beautiful and just. Yet I fancy that if a man appears of capacity sufficient to shake off and break through and escape from all these conventions, he will trample under foot our ordinances and charms and spells, all this mass of unnatural legislation; our slave will stand forth revealed as our master and the light of natural justice will shine forth!

JOHN CALVIN

Original Sin

John Calvin was born in Noyon, France, in 1509. Intended for the priesthood, he was persuaded to study law at the University of Paris. His early works indicate an interest in Renaissance humanism. Luther's work in Germany had inaugurated the Reformation. In 1534, Calvin left France to avoid prosecution for heresy and settled in Switzerland. In 1536 he published the first edition of The Institutes of the Christian Religion, *a sort of manifesto for Protestants. As chief pastor of Geneva, he became the head of a theocratic despotism, wrote voluminously, and enforced a harsh puritanical code of behavior. He died in 1564.*

To remove all uncertainty and misunderstanding on this subject, let us define original sin. It is not my intention to discuss all the definitions given by writers; I shall only produce one, which I think perfectly consistent with the truth. Original sin, therefore, appears to be a hereditary depravity and corruption of our nature, diffused through all the parts of the soul, rendering us obnoxious to the divine wrath and producing in us those works which the Scripture calls "works of the flesh."[1] And this is indeed what Paul frequently denominates "sin." The works which proceed thence, such as adulteries, fornications, thefts, hatreds, murders, revelings, he calls in the same manner "fruits of sin," although they are also called "sins" in many passages of Scripture and even by himself. These two things, therefore, should be distinctly observed: first, that our nature being so totally vitiated and depraved, we are, on account of this very corruption, considered as convicted and justly condemned in the sight of God, to whom nothing is acceptable but righteousness, innocence, and purity. And this liableness to punishment does not arise from the delinquency of another; for when it is said that the sin of Adam renders us obnoxious to the divine judgment, it is not to be understood as if we, though innocent, were undeservedly loaded with the guilt of his sin, but, because we are all subject to a curse in consequence of his transgression,

From John Calvin, *Institutes of the Christian Religion,* 3 vols., trans. from the Latin and collated with the author's last edition in French by John Allen (London, 1813), Bk. II, Chap. 1; Book III, Chaps. 6 and 10.

[1] Gal. 5:19.

he is therefore said to have involved us in guilt. Nevertheless we derive from him not only the punishment but also the pollution to which the punishment is justly due. Wherefore Augustine, though he frequently calls it the sin of another the more clearly to indicate its transmission to us by propagation, yet at the same time also asserts it properly to belong to every individual. And the Apostle himself expressly declares that "death has therefore passed upon all men, for that all have sinned" [2]—that is, have been involved in original sin and defiled with its blemishes. And therefore infants themselves, as they bring their condemnation into the world with them, are rendered obnoxious to punishment by their own sinfulness, not by the sinfulness of another. For though they have not yet produced the fruits of their iniquity, yet they have the seed of it within them; even their whole nature is, as it were, a seed of sin, and therefore cannot but be odious and abominable to God. Whence it follows that it is properly accounted sin in the sight of God because there could be no guilt without crime. The other thing to be remarked is that this depravity never ceases in us but is perpetually producing new fruits, those works of the flesh which we have before described, like the emission of flame and sparks from a heated furnace or like the streams of water from a never-failing spring. Wherefore those who have defined original sin as a privation of the original righteousness which we ought to possess, though they comprise the whole of the subject, yet have not used language sufficiently expressive of its operation and influence. For our nature is not only destitute of all good, but is so fertile in all evils that it cannot remain inactive. Those who have called it "concupiscence" have used an expression not improper, if it were only added, which is far from being conceded by most persons, that everything in man—the understanding and will, the soul and body—is polluted and engrossed by this concupiscence; or, to express it more briefly, that man is of himself nothing else but concupiscence. . . .

Wherefore I have asserted that sin has possessed all the powers of the soul since Adam departed from the fountain of righteousness. For man has not only been ensnared by the inferior appetites, but abominable impiety has seized the very citadel of his mind, and pride has penetrated into the inmost recesses of his heart; so that it is weak and foolish to restrict the corruption which has proceeded thence to what are called the sensual affections, or

[2] Rom. 5:12.

to call it an incentive which allures, excites, and attracts to sin only what they style the sensual part. In this the grossest ignorance has been discovered by Peter Lombard, who, when investigating the seat of it, says that it is in the flesh, according to the testimony of Paul,[3] not indeed exclusively, but because it principally appears in the flesh; as though Paul designated only a part of the soul and not the whole of our nature, which is opposed to supernatural grace. Now Paul removes every doubt by informing us that the corruption resides not in one part only, but that there is nothing pure and uncontaminated by its mortal infection. For, when arguing respecting corrupt nature, he not only condemns the inordinate motions of the appetites, but principally insists on the blindness of the mind and the depravity of the heart;[4] and the third chapter of his Epistle to the Romans is nothing but a description of original sin. This appears more evident from our renovation. For "the Spirit," which is opposed to "the whole man" and "the flesh," not only denotes the grave which corrects the inferior or sensual part of the soul, but comprehends a complete reformation of all its powers. And therefore Paul not only enjoins us to mortify our sensual appetites but exhorts us to be renewed in the spirit of our mind;[5] and in another place he directs us to be transformed by the renewing of our mind.[6] Whence it follows that that part which principally displays the excellence and dignity of the soul is not only wounded but so corrupted that it requires not merely to be healed but to receive a new nature. How far sin occupies both the mind and the heart we shall presently see. My intention here was only to hint, in a brief way, that man is so totally overwhelmed, as with a deluge, that no part is free from sin; and therefore that whatever proceeds from him is accounted sin; as Paul says that all the affections or thoughts of the flesh are enmity against God, and therefore death.[7] . . .

Now let those who are of opinion that the philosophers have the only just and orderly systems of moral philosophy show me, in any of their works, a more excellent economy than that which I have stated. When they intend to exhort us to the sublimest virtue, they advance no argument but that we ought to live agreeably to

[3] Rom. 7:18.
[4] Eph. 4:17, 18.
[5] Eph. 4:23.
[6] Rom. 12:2.
[7] Rom. 8:6, 7.

nature; but the Scripture deduces its exhortation from the true source when it not only enjoins us to refer our life to God the author of it, to whom it belongs, but, after having taught us that we are degenerated from the original state in which we were created, adds that Christ, by whom we have been reconciled to God, is proposed to us as an example, whose character we should exhibit in our lives. What can be required more efficacious than this one consideration? Indeed, what can be required besides? For if the Lord has adopted us as his sons on this condition—that we exhibit in our life an imitation of Christ, the bond of our adoption—unless we addict and devote ourselves to righteousness, we not only most perfidiously revolt from our Creator but also abjure him as our Saviour. The Scripture derives matter of exhortation from all the blessings of God which it recounts to us, and from all the parts of our salvation. It argues that since God has discovered himself as a Father to us, we must be convicted of the basest ingratitude unless we, on our part, manifest ourselves to be his children; that since Christ has purified us in the laver of his blood, and has communicated this purification by baptism, it does not become us to be defiled with fresh pollution; that since he has united us to his body, we should, as his members, solicitously beware lest we asperse ourselves with any blemish or disgrace; that since he who is our Head has ascended to heaven, we ought to divest ourselves of all terrestrial affection and aspire thither with all our soul; that since the Holy Spirit has dedicated us as temples to God, we should use our utmost exertions that the glory of God may be displayed by us and ought not to allow ourselves to be profaned with the pollution of sin; that since both our soul and our body are destined to heavenly incorruption and a never-fading crown, we ought to exert our most strenuous efforts to preserve them pure and uncorrupt till the day of the Lord. These, I say, are the best foundations for the proper regulation of the life, such as we cannot find in the philosophers, who, in the recommendation of virtue, never rise above the natural dignity of man. . . .

The Human Vocation

Yet I would not insist upon it as absolutely necessary that the manners of a Christian should breathe nothing but the perfect gospel—which, nevertheless, ought both to be wished and to be aimed at. But I do not so rigorously require evangelical perfection as not to acknowledge as a Christian one who has not yet attained to it; for then all would be excluded from the Church, since no man can be found who is not still at a great distance from it, and many have hitherto made but a very small progress whom it would, nevertheless, be unjust to reject. What then? Let us set before our eyes that mark to which alone our pursuit must be directed. Let that be prescribed as the goal toward which we must earnestly tend. For it is not lawful for you to make such a compromise with God as to undertake a part of the duties prescribed to you in his word and to omit part of them at your own pleasure. For, in the first place, he everywhere recommends integrity as a principal branch of his worship, by which he intends a sincere simplicity of heart, free from all guile and falsehood, the opposite of which is a double heart; as though it has been said that the beginning of a life of uprightness is spiritual, when the internal affection of the mind is unfeignedly devoted to God in the cultivation of holiness and righteousness. But since no man in this terrestrial and corporeal prison has strength sufficient to press forward in his course with a due degree of alacrity, and the majority are oppressed with such great debility that they stagger and halt and even creep on the ground, and so make very inconsiderable advances—let us everyone proceed according to our small ability and prosecute the journey we have begun. No man will be so unhappy but that he may every day make some progress, however small. Therefore let us not cease to strive, that we may be incessantly advancing in the way of the Lord; nor let us despair on account of the smallness of our success; for however our success may not correspond to our wishes, yet our labor is not lost when this day surpasses the preceding one; provided that, with sincere simplicity, we keep our end in view, and press forward to the goal, not practicing self-adulation nor indulging our own evil propensities, but perpetually exerting our endeavors after increasing degrees of amelioration, till we shall have arrived at a perfection of goodness, which, indeed, we seek and pursue as long as we live, and shall then attain, when, divested of all corporeal infirmity, we shall be admitted by God into complete communion with him. . . .

Lastly, it is to be remarked that the Lord commands every one of us, in all the actions of life, to regard his vocation. For he knows with what great inquietude the human mind is inflamed, with what desultory levity it is hurried hither and thither, and how insatiable in its ambition to grasp different things at once. Therefore, to prevent universal confusion being produced by our folly and temerity, he has appointed to all their particular duties in different spheres of life. And that no one might rashly transgress the limits prescribed, he has styled such spheres of life "vocations," or "callings." Every individual's line of life, therefore, is, as it were, a post assigned him by the Lord, that he may not wander about in uncertainty all his days. And so necessary is this distinction that in his sight all our actions are estimated according to it, and often very differently from the sentence of human reason and philosophy. There is no exploit esteemed more honorable, even among philosophers, than to deliver our country from tyranny; but the voice of the celestial Judge openly condemns the private man who lays violent hands on a tyrant. It is not my design, however, to stay to enumerate examples. It is sufficient if we know that the principle and foundation of right conduct in every case are the vocation of the Lord, and that he who disregards it will never keep the right way in the duties of his station. He may sometimes, perhaps, achieve something apparently laudable; but however it may appear in the eyes of men, it will be rejected at the throne of God; besides which, there will be no consistency between the various parts of his life. Our life, therefore, will then be best regulated when it is directed to this mark, since no one will be impelled by his own temerity to attempt more than is compatible with his calling, because he will know that it is unlawful to transgress the bounds assigned him. He that is in obscurity will lead a private life without discontent so as not to desert the station in which God has placed him. It will also be no small alleviation of his cares, labors, troubles, and other burdens when a man knows that in all these things he has God for his guide. The magistrate will execute his office with greater pleasure, the father of a family will confine himself to his duty with more satisfaction, and all, in their respective spheres of life, will bear and surmount the inconveniences, cares, disappointments, and anxieties which befall them, when they shall be persuaded that every individual has his burden laid upon him by God. Hence also will arise peculiar consolation, since there will be no employment so mean and sordid (provided we follow our vocation) as not to appear truly respectable and be deemed highly important in the sight of God.

ALBERT CAMUS

Encounter with the Absurd

Albert Camus, winner of the Nobel Prize for literature in 1957, was born in Mondovi, Algeria, in 1913 and spent the early years of his life in North Africa. After taking a degree in philosophy, he worked at various jobs, including the running of a theatrical company in the thirties. Later he became a journalist and traveled to the French mainland, where he was active in the underground during the war as anonymous editor of the résistance *newspaper* Combat. *His philosophical essay* The Myth of Sisyphus *and his first novel,* The Stranger, *were published in occupied France of 1942. Camus's works include two additional novels,* The Plague *(1947) and* The Fall *(1957); Exile and the Kingdom, a volume of short stories; plays* (Caligula and Three Other Plays, *published here in 1958), and philosophical essays, collected in* The Rebel *(1951) and* Resistance, Rebellion and Death, *published after his death in an automobile accident in 1960.*

All great deeds and all great thoughts have a ridiculous beginning. Great works are often born on a street-corner or in a restaurant's revolving door. So it is with absurdity. The absurd world more than others derives its nobility from that abject birth. In certain situations, replying "nothing" when asked what one is thinking about may be pretense in a man. Those who are loved are well aware of this. But if that reply is sincere, if it symbolizes that odd state of soul in which the void becomes eloquent, in which the chain of daily gestures is broken, in which the heart vainly seeks the link that will connect it again, then it is as it were the first sign of absurdity.

It happens that the stage sets collapse. Rising, streetcar, four hours in the office or the factory, meal, streetcar, four hours of work, meal, sleep, and Monday Tuesday Wednesday Thursday Friday and Saturday according to the same rhythm—this path is easily followed most of the time. But one day the "why" arises and everything begins in that weariness tinged with amazement. "Begins" —this is important. Weariness comes at the end of the acts of a

---

From Albert Camus, *The Myth of Sisyphus*, trans. Justin O'Brien (New York: Alfred A. Knopf, 1955), pp. 12–13, 16–21, 51–53, 57–58, 60–62, *passim*. Used by permission of Knopf, and of Hamish Hamilton, Ltd., London.

mechanical life, but at the same time it inaugurates the impulse of consciousness. It awakens consciousness and provokes what follows. What follows is the gradual return into the chain or it is the definitive awakening. At the end of the awakening comes, in time, the consequence: suicide or recovery. In itself weariness has something sickening about it. Here, I must conclude that it is good. For everything begins with consciousness and nothing is worth anything except through it.

At the heart of all beauty lies something inhuman, and these hills, the softness of the sky, the outline of these trees at this very minute lose the illusory meaning with which we had clothed them, henceforth more remote than a lost paradise. The primitive hostility of the world rises up to face us across millennia. For a second we cease to understand it because for centuries we have understood in it solely the images and designs that we had attributed to it beforehand, because henceforth we lack the power to make use of that artifice. The world evades us because it becomes itself again. That stage scenery masked by habit becomes again what it is. It withdraws at a distance from us. Just as there are days when under the familiar face of a woman, we see as a stranger her we had loved months or years ago, perhaps we shall come even to desire what suddenly leaves us so alone. But the time has not yet come. Just one thing: that denseness and that strangeness of the world is the absurd.

Men, too, secrete the inhuman. At certain moments of lucidity, the mechanical aspect of their gestures, their meaningless pantomime makes silly everything that surrounds them. A man is talking on the telephone behind a glass partition; you cannot hear him, but you see his incomprehensible dumb show: you wonder why he is alive. This discomfort in the face of man's own inhumanity, this incalculable tumble before the image of what we are, this "nausea," as a writer of today calls it, is also the absurd. Likewise, the stranger who at certain seconds comes to meet us in a mirror, the familiar and yet alarming brother we encounter in our own photographs is also the absurd. . . .

I come at last to death and to the attitude we have toward it. On this point everything has been said and it is only proper to avoid pathos. Yet one will never be sufficiently surprised that everyone lives as if no one "knew." This is because in reality there is no experience of death. Properly speaking, nothing has been experienced but what has been lived and made conscious. Here, it is barely possible to speak of the experience of others' deaths. It is a substitute, an illusion, and it never quite convinces us. That melancholy convention cannot be persuasive. The horror comes in reality from the mathematical aspect of the event. If time frightens us, this is because it works out the problem and the solution comes afterward. All the pretty speeches about the soul will have their contrary convincingly proved, at least for a time. From this inert body on which a slap makes no mark the soul has disappeared. This elementary and definitive aspect of the adventure constitutes the absurd feeling. Under the fatal lighting of that destiny, its uselessness becomes evident. No code of ethics and no effort are justifiable *a priori* in the face of the cruel mathematics that command our condition. . . .

Understanding the world for a man is reducing it to the human, stamping it with his seal. The cat's universe is not the universe of the anthill. The truism "All thought is anthropomorphic" has no other meaning. Likewise, the mind that aims to understand reality can consider itself satisfied only by reducing it to terms of thought. If man realized that the universe like him can love and suffer, he would be reconciled. If thought discovered in the shimmering mirrors of phenomena eternal relations capable of summing them up and summing themselves up in a single principle, then would be seen an intellectual joy of which the myth of the blessed would be but a ridiculous imitation. That nostalgia for unity, that appetite for the absolute illustrates the essential impulse of the human drama. But the fact of that nostalgia's existence does not imply that it is to be immediately satisfied. . . .

With the exception of professional rationalists, today people despair of true knowledge. If the only significant history of human thought were to be written, it would have to be the history of its successive regrets and its impotences.

Of whom and of what indeed can I say: "I know that!" This heart within me I can feel, and I judge that it exists. This world I can touch, and I likewise judge that it exists. There ends all my knowledge, and the rest is construction. For if I try to seize this self of which I feel sure, if I try to define and to summarize it, it is nothing but water slipping through my fingers. I can sketch one by one all the aspects it is able to assume, all those likewise that have been attributed to it, this upbringing, this origin, this ardor or these silences, this nobility or this vileness. But aspects cannot be added up. This very heart which is mine will forever remain indefinable to me. Between the certainty I have of my existence and the content I try to give to that assurance, the gap will never be filled. Forever I shall be a stranger to myself. . . .

Hence the intelligence, too, tells me in its way that this world is absurd. . . . In this unintelligible and limited universe, man's fate henceforth assumes its meaning. A horde of irrationals has sprung up and surrounds him until his ultimate end. In his recovered and now studied lucidity, the feeling of the absurd becomes clear and definite. I said that the world is absurd, but I was too hasty. This world in itself is not reasonable, that is all that can be said. But what is absurd is the confrontation of this irrational and the wild longing for clarity whose call echoes in the human heart. The absurd depends as much on man as on the world. . . .

I don't know whether this world has a meaning that transcends it. But I know that I do not know that meaning and that it is impossible for me just now to know it. What can a meaning outside my condition mean to me? I can understand only in human terms. What I touch, what resists me—that is what I understand. And these two certainties—my appetite for the absolute and for unity and the impossibility of reducing this world to a rational and reasonable principle—I also know that I cannot reconcile them. What other truth can I admit without lying, without bringing in a hope I lack and which means nothing within the limits of my condition?

If I were a tree among trees, a cat among animals, this life would have a meaning, or rather this problem would not arise, for I should belong to this world. I should *be* this world to which I am now opposed by my whole consciousness and my whole insistence upon familiarity. This ridiculous reason is what sets me in opposition to all creation. I cannot cross it out with a stroke of the pen. What I believe to be true I must therefore preserve. What seems to me so obvious, even against me, I must support. And what constitutes the basis of that conflict, of that break between the world and my mind, but the awareness of it? If therefore I want to preserve it, I can through a constant awareness, ever revived, ever alert. This is what, for the moment, I must remember. . . .

Let us insist again on the method: it is a matter of persisting. At

Encounter with the Absurd / 39

a certain point on his path the absurd man is tempted. History is not lacking in either religions or prophets, even without gods. He is asked to leap. All he can reply is that he doesn't fully understand, that it is not obvious. Indeed, he does not want to do anything but what he fully understands. He is assured that this is the sin of pride, but he does not understand the notion of sin; that perhaps hell is in store, but he has not enough imagination to visualize that strange future; that he is losing immortal life, but that seems to him an idle consideration. An attempt is made to get him to admit his guilt. He feels innocent. To tell the truth, that is all he feels—his irreparable innocence. This is what allows him everything. Hence, what he demands of himself is to live *solely* with what he knows, to accommodate himself to what is, and to bring in nothing that is not certain. He is told that nothing is. But this at least is a certainty. And it is with this that he is concerned: he wants to find out if it is possible to live *without appeal*. . . .

Before encountering the absurd, the everyday man lives with aims, a concern for the future or for justification (with regard to whom or what is not the question). He weighs his chances, he counts on "someday," his retirement or the labor of his sons. He still thinks that something in his life can be directed. In truth, he acts as if he were free, even if all the facts make a point of contradicting that liberty. But after the absurd, everything is upset. That idea that "I am," my way of acting as if everything has a meaning (even if, on occasion, I said that nothing has)—all that is given the lie in vertiginous fashion by the absurdity of a possible death. Thinking of the future, establishing aims for oneself, having preferences—all this presupposes a belief in freedom, even if one occasionally ascertains that one doesn't feel it. But at that moment I am well aware that that higher liberty, that freedom *to be*, which alone can serve as basis for a truth, does not exist. Death is there as the only reality. . . .

But at the same time the absurd man realizes that hitherto he was bound to that postulate of freedom on the illusion of which he was living. In a certain sense, that hampered him. To the extent to which he imagined a purpose to his life, he adapted himself to the demands of a purpose to be achieved and became the slave of his liberty. Thus I could not act otherwise than as the father (or the engineer or the leader of a nation, or the post-office subclerk) that I am preparing to be. . . .

The absurd enlightens me on this point: there is no future. Henceforth, this is the reason for my inner freedom. . . .

But what does life mean in such a universe? Nothing else for the moment but indifference to the future and a desire to use up everything that is given. Belief in the meaning of life always implies a scale of values, a choice, our preferences. Belief in the absurd, according to our definitions, teaches the contrary. But this is worth examining.

Knowing whether or not one can live *without appeal* is all that interests me. I do not want to get out of my depth. This aspect of life being given me, can I adapt myself to it? Now, faced with this particular concern, belief in the absurd is tantamount to substituting the quantity of experiences for the quality. If I convince myself that this life has no other aspect than that of the absurd, if I feel that its whole equilibrium depends on that perpetual opposition between my conscious revolt and the darkness in which it struggles, if I admit that my freedom has no meaning except in relation to its limited fate, then I must say that what counts is not the best of living but the most living. . . .

On the one hand the absurd teaches that all experiences are unimportant, and on the other it urges toward the greatest quantity of experiences. How, then, can one fail to do as so many of those men I was speaking of earlier—choose the form of life that brings us the most possible of that human matter, thereby introducing a scale of values that on the other hand one claims to reject?

But again it is the absurd and its contradictory life that teaches us. For the mistake is thinking that that quantity of experiences depends on the circumstances of our life when it depends solely on us. Here we have to be over-simple. To two men living the same number of years, the world always provides the same sum of experiences. It is up to us to be conscious of them. Being aware of one's life, one's revolt, one's freedom, and to the maximum, is living, and to the maximum. Where lucidity dominates, the scale of values becomes useless.

THOMAS HOBBES

Of the State of Men Without Civil Society

Thomas Hobbes was born in 1588 and educated at Oxford. He spent a large part of his life as a tutor, friend, and adviser to members of the great Cavendish family and so secured the leisure necessary for his writing. The discoveries of Galileo, whom he met in 1636, impressed him with the need for a philosophical system which would be based, like the new science, on the principles of matter and motion. His pro-royalist sympathies led him to take refuge in France before the outbreak of the English civil war in 1642. In Paris, he became tutor to the Prince of Wales, later Charles II. With the publication of De Cive *(1642) and* Leviathan *(1651) Hobbes fell out of favor with the royalists and returned to England where, under Cromwell and later under Charles II, he continued to write voluminously on a variety of topics. He died in 1679.*

The faculties of human nature may be reduced unto four kinds; bodily strength, experience, reason, passion. Taking the beginning of this following doctrine from these, we will declare in the first place what manner of inclinations men who are endued with these faculties bear towards each other, and whether, and by what faculty they are born, apt for society, and to preserve themselves against mutual violence; then proceeding, we will shew what advice was necessary to be taken for this business, and what are the conditions of society, or of human peace; that is to say, (changing the words only) what are the fundamental laws of nature.

The greatest part of those men who have written aught concerning commonwealths, either suppose, or require us, or beg of us to believe, that man is a creature born fit[1] for society. The Greeks

From *De Cive,* or *The Citizen,* ed. with an introduction by Sterling P. Lamprecht (New York: Appleton-Century-Crofts Div. of Meredith Publishing Co., 1949), pp. 63, 64–65, 175, 177–180, *passim.*

[1] Since we now see actually a constituted society among men, and none living out of it, since we discern all desirous of congress, and mutual correspondence, it may seem a wonderful kind of stupidity, to lay in the very threshold of this doctrine, such a stumbling block before the readers, as to deny man to be born fit for society. Therefore I must more plainly say, that it is true indeed, that to man, by nature, or as man, that is, as soon as he is

call him ζῷον πολιτικόν;[2] and on this foundation they so build up the doctrine of civil society, as if for the preservation of peace, and the government of mankind, there were nothing else necessary, than that men should agree to make certain covenants and conditions together, which themselves should then call laws. Which axiom, though received by most, is yet certainly false, and an error proceeding from our too slight contemplation of human nature. For they who shall more narrowly look into the causes for which men come together, and delight in each other's company, shall easily find that this happens not because naturally it could happen no otherwise, but by accident. For if by nature one man should love another (that is) as man, there could no reason be returned why every man should not equally love every man, as being equally man, or why he should rather frequent those whose society affords him honour or profit. We do not therefore by nature seek society for its own sake, but that we may receive some honour or profit from it; these we desire primarily, that secondarily. How, by what advice, men do meet, will be best known by observing those things which they do when they are met. For if they meet for traffic, it is plain every man regards not his fellow, but his business; if to discharge some office, a cerain market-friendship is begotten, which hath more of jealousy in it than true love, and whence factions sometimes may arise, but good will never; if for

---

born, solitude is an enemy; for infants have need of others to help them to live, and those of riper years to help them to live well, wherefore I deny that men (even nature compelling) desire to come together. But civil societies are not mere meetings, but bonds, to the making whereof, faith and compacts are necessary: the virtue whereof to children, and fools, and the profit whereof to those who have not yet tasted the miseries which accompany its defects, is altogether unknown; whence it happens, that those, because they know not what society is, cannot enter into it; these, because ignorant of the benefit it brings, care not for it. Manifest therefore it is, that all men, because they are born in infancy, are born unapt for society. Many also (perhaps most men) either through defect of mind, of want of education, remain unfit during the whole course of their lives; yet have they, infants as well as those of riper years, a human nature; wherefore man is made fit for society not by nature, but by education. Furthermore, although man were born in such a condition as to desire it, it follows not, that he therefore were born fit to enter into it; for it is one thing to desire, another to be in capacity fit for what we desire; for even they, who through their pride, will not stoop to equal condition, without which there can be no society, do yet desire it.

[2] "The political animal."—Ed.

pleasure, and recreation of mind, every man is wont to please himself most with those things which stir up laughter, whence he may (according to the nature of that which is ridiculous) by comparison of another man's defects and infirmities, pass the more current in his own opinion; and although this be sometimes innocent and without offence, yet it is manifest they are not so much delighted with the society, as their own vain glory. . . .

But if it so happen, that being met, they pass their time in relating some stories, and one of them begins to tell one which concerns himself; instantly every one of the rest most greedily desires to speak of himself too; if one relate some wonder, the rest will tell you miracles, if they have them, if not, they will feign them. Lastly, that I may say somewhat of them who pretend to be wiser than others; if they meet to talk of philosophy, look how many men, so many would be esteemed masters, or else they not only love not their fellows, but even persecute them with hatred. So clear is it by experience to all men who a little more narrowly consider human affairs, that all free congress ariseth either from mutual poverty, or from vain glory, whence the parties met, endeavour to carry with them either some benefit, or to leave behind them that same εὐδοκιμεῖν [3] some esteem and honour with those, with whom they have been conversant. The same is also collected by reason out of the definitions themselves, of will, good, honour, profitable. For when we voluntarily contract society, in all manner of society we look after the object of the will, that is, that, which every one of those who gather together, propounds to himself for good. Now whatsoever seems good, is pleasant, and relates either to the senses, or the mind. But all the mind's pleasure is either glory, (or to have a good opinion of one's self) or refers to glory in the end; the rest are sensual, or conducing to sensuality, which may be all comprehended under the word conveniences. All society therefore is either for gain, or for glory; that is, not so much for love of our fellows, as for the love of ourselves. But no society can be great, or lasting, which begins from vain glory; because that glory is like honour, if all men have it, no man hath it, for they consist in comparison and precellence; neither doth the society of others advance any whit the cause of my glorying in myself; for every man must account himself, such as he can make himself,

[3] Good repute.—Ed.

without the help of others. But though the benefits of this life may be much farthered by mutual help, since yet those may be better attained to by dominion, than by the society of others: I hope no body will doubt but that men would much more greedily be carried by nature, if all fear were removed, to obtain dominion, than to gain society. We must therefore resolve, that the original of all great and lasting societies consisted not in the mutual good will men had towards each other, but in the mutual fear [4] they had of each other. . . .

All men in the state of nature have a desire and will to hurt, but not proceeding from the same cause, neither equally to be condemned. For one man, according to that natural equality which is among us, permits as much to others, as he assumes to himself (which is an argument of a temperate man, and one that rightly values his power). Another, supposing himself above others, will have a license to do what he lists, and challenges respect and honour, as due to him before others, (which is an argument of a fiery spirit). This man's will to hurt ariseth from vain glory, and the false esteem he hath of his own strength; the other's, from the necessity of defending himself, his liberty, and his goods, against this man's violence. . . .

But the most frequent reason why men desire to hurt each other, ariseth hence, that many men at the same time have an appetite to the same thing; which yet very often they can neither enjoy in common, nor yet divide it; whence it follows that the strongest must have it, and who is strongest must be decided by the sword.

[4] It is objected: it is so improbable that men should grow into civil societies out of fear, that if they had been afraid, they would not have endured each other's looks. They presume, I believe, that to fear is nothing else than to be affrighted. I comprehend in this word fear, a certain foresight of future evil; neither do I conceive flight the sole property of fear, but to distrust, suspect, take heed, provide so that they may not fear, is also incident to the fearful. They who go to sleep, shut their doors; they who travel, carry their swords with them, because they fear thieves. Kingdoms guard their coasts and frontiers with forts and castles; cities are compact with walls, and all for fear of neighbouring kingdoms and towns; even the strongest armies, and most accomplished for fight, yet sometimes parley for peace, as fearing each other's power, and lest they might be overcome. It is through fear that men secure themselves, by flight indeed, and in corners, if they think they cannot escape otherwise; but for the most part by arms and defensive weapons; whence it happens, that daring to come forth, they know each other's spirits; but then, if they fight, civil society ariseth from the victory, if they agree, from their agreement.

OF THE CAUSES AND FIRST BEGINNING OF CIVIL GOVERNMENT

It is of itself manifest, that the actions of men proceed from the will, and the will from hope and fear, insomuch as when they shall see a greater good, or less evil, likely to happen to them by the breach, than observation of the laws, they will wittingly violate them. The hope therefore which each man hath of his security and self-preservation, consists in this, that by force or craft he may disappoint his neighbour, either openly, or by stratagem. Whence we may understand, that the natural laws, though well understood, do not instantly secure any man in their practice, and consequently, that as long as there is no caution had from the invasion of others, there remains to every man that same primitive right of self-defence, by such means as either he can or will make use of, that is, a right to all things, or the right of war. And it is sufficient for the fulfilling of the natural law, that a man be prepared in mind to embrace peace when it may be had. . . .

Since therefore the exercise of the natural law is necessary for the preservation of peace, and that for the exercise of the natural law security is no less necessary, it is worth the considering what that is which affords such a security. For this matter nothing else can be imagined, but that each man provide himself of such meet helps, as the invasion of one on the other may be rendered so dangerous, as either of them may think it better to refrain, than to meddle. But first, it is plain, that the consent of two or three cannot make good such a security; because that the addition but of one, or some few on the other side, is sufficient to make the victory undoubtedly sure, and heartens the enemy to attack us. It is therefore necessary, to the end the security sought for may be obtained, that the number of them who conspire in a mutual assistance be so great, that the accession of some few to the enemy's party may not prove to them a matter of moment sufficient to assure the victory.

Furthermore, how great soever the number of them is who meet on self-defence, if yet they agree not among themselves of some excellent means whereby to compass this, but every man after his own manner shall make use of his endeavors, nothing will be done; because that, divided in their opinions, they will be a hindrance to each other, or if they agree well enough to some one action through hope of victory, spoil, or revenge, yet afterward through diversity of wits, and counsels, or emulation, and envy, with which men naturally contend, they will be so torn and rent, as they will neither give mutual help, nor desire peace, except they be constrained to it by some common fear. Whence it follows that the consent of many, (which consists in this only, that they direct all their actions to the same end, and the common good), that is to say, that the society proceeding from mutual help only, yields not that security which they seek for, who meet and agree in the exercise of the above-named laws of nature; but that somewhat else must be done, that those who have once consented for the common good, to peace and mutual help, may by fear be restrained, lest afterwards they again dissent, when their private interest shall appear discrepant from the common good. . . .

GOD'S AUTHORITY BASED ON POWER

We have already proved both by reason and testimonies of holy writ, that the estate of nature, that is to say, of absolute liberty, such as is theirs, who neither govern nor are governed, is an anarchy or hostile state; that the precepts whereby to avoid this state, are the laws of nature; that there can be no civil government without a sovereign; and that they who have gotten this sovereign command must be obeyed simply, that is to say, in all things which repugn not the commandments of God. There is this one thing only wanting to the complete understanding of all civil duty, and that is, to know which are the laws and commandments of God. For else we cannot tell whether that which the civil power commands us, be against the laws of God, or not; whence it must necessarily happen, that either by too much obedience to the civil authority, we become stubborn against the divine Majesty; or for fear of sinning against God, we run into disobedience against the civil power. To avoid both these rocks, it is necessary to know the divine laws. Now because the knowledge of the laws depends on the knowledge of the kingdom, we must in what follows speak somewhat concerning the kingdom of God. . . .

God in his natural kingdom hath a right to rule, and to punish those who break his laws, from his sole irresistible power. For all right over others is either from nature, or from contract. How the right of governing springs from contract, we have already showed. And the same right is derived from nature, in this very thing, that it is not by nature taken away. For when by nature all men had a right over all things, every man had a right of ruling over all as ancient as nature itself. But the reason why this was abolished among men, was no other but mutual fear, reason, namely, dictating that they must forego that right for the preservation of mankind, because the equality of men among themselves, according to their strength and natural powers, was necessarily accompanied with war, and with war joins the destruction of mankind. Now if any man had so far exceeded the rest in power, that all of them with joined forces could not have resisted him, there had been no cause why he should part with that right which nature had given him. The right therefore of dominion over all the rest, would have remained with him, by reason of that excess of power whereby he could have preserved both himself and them. They therefore whose power cannot be resisted, and by consequence God Almighty, derives his right of sovereignty from the power itself. And as oft as God punisheth or slays a sinner, although he therefore punish him because he sinned, yet may we not say that he could not justly have punished or killed him although he had not sinned. Neither, if the will of God in punishing may perhaps have regard to some sin antecedent, doth it therefore follow, that the right of afflicting and killing depends not on divine power, but on men's sins.

That question made famous by the disputations of the ancients, why evil things befell the good, and good things the evil, is the same with this of ours, by what right God dispenseth good and evil things unto men. And with its difficulty, it not only staggers the faith of the vulgar concerning the divine providence, but also of philosophers, and which is more, even of holy men. Psalm lxxiii. 1, 2, 3: *Truly God is good to Israel, even to such as are of a clean heart; but as for me, my feet were almost gone, my steps had well nigh slipped. And why? I was grieved at the wicked; I do also see the ungodly in such prosperity.* And how bitterly did Job expostulate with God, that being just, he should yet be afflicted with so many calamities? God himself with open voice resolved this difficulty in the case of Job, and hath confirmed his right by arguments drawn not from Job's sin, but from his own power. For Job and his friends had argued so among themselves, that they would needs make him guilty, because he was punished; and he would reprove their accusation by arguments fetched from his own innocence. But God, when he had heard both him and them, refutes his expostulation, not by condemning him of injustice or any sin, but by declaring his own power (Job xxxviii. 4): *Where wast thou* (says he) *when I laid the foundation of the earth, & etc.* . . .

Now if God have the right of sovereignty from his power, it is manifest, that the obligations of yielding him obedience lies on men by reason of their weakness.[5] For that obligation which rises from contract, of which we have spoken in Chapter II, can have no place here, where the right of ruling (no covenant passing between) rises only from nature. But there are two species of natural obligation, one, when liberty is taken away by corporal impediments, according to which we say that heaven and earth, and all creatures, do obey the common laws of their creation; the other, when it is taken away by hope or fear, according to which the weaker, despairing of his own power to resist, cannot but yield to the stronger. From this last kind of obligation, that is to say, from fear, or conscience of our own weakness (in respect of the divine power), it comes to pass, that we are obliged to obey God in his natural kingdom; reason dictating to all, acknowledging the divine power and providence, that there is no kicking against the pricks.

[5] If this shall seem hard to any man, I desire him with a silent thought to consider, if there were two Omnipotents, whether either were bound to obey. I believe he will confess that neither is bound. If this be true, then it is also true that what I have set down; that men are subject unto God, because they are not omnipotent. And truly our Saviour admonishing Paul, (who at that time was an enemy to the Church) that he should not kick against the pricks, seems to require obedience from him for this cause, because he had not power enough to resist.

FRIEDRICH NIETZSCHE

Beyond Good and Evil

Friedrich Nietzsche was born in Germany in 1844, the son of a Protestant minister. In 1869, after completing his studies at the universities of Bonn and Leipzig, he was appointed professor of classical philology at the University of Basel and became a Swiss subject. At Basel he taught Greek literature and philosophy and became a close friend and admirer of Richard Wagner (with whom he later quarreled). He published his first book, The Birth of Tragedy from the Spirit of Music, *in 1872. Nietzsche's health had never been good and after ten years at Basel, he was forced to retire. For the next ten years Nietzsche lived in Swiss health resorts, traveled, studied, and devoted himself to his writing, which sharply criticized traditional religion and morality. His major works, all written during this period, included* Thus Spake Zarathustra *(1883–85),* Beyond Good and Evil *(1886), and* The Genealogy of Morals *(1887). In 1889, only one year after first achieving public recognition, he suffered a mental breakdown and remained insane until his death in 1900.*

Apart from the value of such assertions as "there is a categorical imperative in us," one can always ask: What does such an assertion indicate about him who makes it? There are systems of morals which are meant to justify their author in the eyes of other people; other systems of morals are meant to tranquillise him, and make him self-satisfied; with other systems he wants to crucify and humble himself; with others he wishes to take revenge; with others to conceal himself; with others to glorify himself and gain superiority and distinction;—this system of morals helps its author to forget, that system makes him, or something of him, forgotten; many a moralist would like to exercise power and creative arbitrariness over mankind; many another, perhaps, Kant especially, gives us to understand by his morals that "what is estimable in me, is that I know how to obey—and with you it *shall* not be otherwise than with me!" In short, systems of morals are only a *sign-language of the emotions*. . . .

From Friedrich Nietzsche, *Beyond Good and Evil*, trans. Helen Zimmern, in *The Philosophy of Nietzsche* (New York: Modern Library, Inc., 1927), pp. 475–476, 532–534, 487, 489, 486, 476, 529–532, *passim*. Used by permission of George Allen & Unwin Ltd, London.

I hope to be forgiven for discovering that all moral philosophy hitherto has been tedious and has belonged to the soporific appliances—and that "virtue," in my opinion, has been *more* injured by the *tediousness* of its advocates than by anything else; at the same time, however, I would not wish to overlook their general usefulness. It is desirable that as few people as possible should reflect upon morals, and consequently it is *very* desirable that morals should not some day become interesting! But let us not be afraid! Things still remain today as they have always been: I see no one in Europe who has (or *discloses*) an idea of the fact that philosophising concerning morals might be conducted in a dangerous, captious, and ensnaring manner—that *calamity* might be involved therein. Observe, for example, the indefatigable, inevitable English utilitarians: how ponderously and respectably they stalk on, stalk along (a Homeric metaphor expresses it better) in the footsteps of Bentham, just as he had already stalked in the footsteps of the respectable Helvétius! . . . In effect, the old English vice called *cant*, which is *moral Tartuffism*, has insinuated itself also into these moralists (whom one must certainly read with an eye to their motives if one *must* read them), concealed this time under the new form of the scientific spirit; moreover, there is not absent from them a secret struggle with the pangs of conscience, from which a race of former Puritans must naturally suffer, in all their scientific tinkering with morals. (Is not a moralist the opposite of a Puritan? That is to say, as a thinker who regards morality as questionable, as worthy of interrogation, in short, as a problem? Is moralising not—immoral?) In the end, they all want *English* morality to be recognised as authoritative, inasmuch as mankind, or the "general utility," or "the happiness of the greatest number,"—no! the happiness of *England*, will be best served thereby. They would like, by all means, to convince themselves that the striving after *English* happiness, I mean after *comfort* and *fashion* (and in the highest instance, a seat in Parliament), is at the same time the true path of virtue; in fact, that in so far as there has been virtue in the world hitherto, it has just consisted in such striving. Not one of those ponderous, conscience-stricken herding-animals (who undertake to advocate the cause of egoism as conducive to the general welfare) wants to have any knowledge or inkling of the facts that the "general welfare" is no ideal, no goal, no notion that can be at all grasped, but is only a nostrum,—that what is fair to one *may not* at all be fair to another, that the requirement of one morality for all is really a detriment to higher men, in short, that there is a *distinction of rank* between man and man, and consequently between morality and morality. . . .

All the systems of morals which address themselves with a view to their "happiness," as it is called—what else are they but suggestions for behaviour adapted to the degree of *danger* from themselves in which the individuals live; recipes for their passions, their good and bad propensities, in so far as such have the Will to Power and would like to play the master; small and great expediencies and elaborations, permeated with the musty odour of old family medicines and old-wife wisdom; all of them grotesque and absurd in their form—because they address themselves to "all," because they generalise where generalisation is not authorised; all of them speaking unconditionally; and taking themselves unconditionally; all of them flavoured not merely with one grain of salt, but rather endurable only, and sometimes even seductive, when they are overspiced and begin to smell dangerously, especially of "the other world?" That is all of little value when estimated intellectually, and is far from being "science," much less "wisdom"; but, repeated once more, and three times repeated, it is expediency expediency, expediency, mixed with stupidity, stupidity, stupidity —whether it be the indifference and statuesque coldness towards the heated folly of the emotions, which the Stoics advised and fostered; or the no-more-laughing and no-more-weeping of Spinoza, the destruction of the emotions by their analysis and vivisection, which he recommended so naïvely; or the lowering of the emotions to an innocent mean at which they may be satisfied, the Aristotelianism of morals; or even morality as the enjoyment of the emotions in a voluntary attenuation and spiritualisation by the symbolism of art, perhaps as music, or as love of God, and of mankind for God's sake—for in religion the passions are once more enfranchised, provided that . . . ; or, finally, even the complaisant and wanton surrender to the emotions, as has been taught by Hafis and Goethe, the bold letting-go of the reins, the spiritual and corporeal *licentia morum* in the exceptional cases of wise old codgers and drunkards, with whom it "no longer has much danger."—This also for the chapter: "Morals as Timidity."

Inasmuch as in all ages, as long as mankind has existed, there have also been human herds (family alliances, communities, tribes, peoples, states, churches), and always a great number who obey in proportion to the small number who command—in view, therefore, of the fact that obedience has been most practised and fostered among mankind hitherto, one may reasonably suppose that, generally speaking, the need thereof is now innate in every one, as a kind of *formal conscience* which gives the command: "Thou shalt unconditionally do something, unconditionally refrain from something"; in short, "Thou shalt." This need tries to satisfy itself and to fill its form with a content; according to its strength, impatience, and eagerness, it at once seizes as an omnivorous appetite with little selection, and accepts whatever is shouted into its ear by all sorts of commanders—parents, teachers, laws, class prejudices, or public opinion. The extraordinary limitation of human development, the hesitation, protractedness, frequent retrogression, and turning thereof, is attributable to the fact that the herd-instinct of obedience is transmitted best, and at the cost of the art of command. If one imagine this instinct increasing to its greatest extent, commanders and independent individuals will finally be lacking altogether; or they will suffer inwardly from a bad conscience, and will have to impose a deception on themselves in the first place in order to be able to command: just as if they also were only obeying. This condition of things actually exists in Europe at present—I call it the moral hypocrisy of the commanding class. They know no other way of protecting themselves from their bad conscience than by playing the role of executors of older and higher orders (of predecessors, of the constitution, of justice, of the law, or of God himself), or they even justify themselves by maxims from the current opinions of the herd, as "first servants of their people," or "instruments of the public weal." On the other hand, the gregarious European man nowadays assumes an air as if he were the only kind of man that is allowable; he glorifies his qualities, such as public spirit, kindness, deference, industry, temperance, modesty, indulgence, sympathy, by virtue of which he is gentle, endurable, and useful to the herd, as the peculiarly human virtues. In cases, however, where it is believed that the leader and bellwether cannot be dispensed with, attempt after attempt is made nowadays to replace commanders by the summing together of clever gregarious men: all representative constitutions, for example, are of this origin. In spite of all, what a blessing, what a deliverance from a weight becoming unendurable, is the appearance of an absolute ruler for these gregarious Europeans—of this fact the effect of the appearance of Napoleon was the last great proof: the history of the influence of Napoleon is almost the history of the higher happiness to which the entire century has attained in its worthiest individuals and periods. . . .

The beast of prey and the man of prey (for instance, Caesar Borgia) are fundamentally misunderstood, "nature" is misunderstood, so long as one seeks a "morbidnesss" in the constitution of these healthiest of all tropical monsters and growths, or even an innate "hell" in them—as almost all moralists have done hitherto. Does it not seem that there is a hatred of the virgin forest and of the tropics among moralists? And that the "tropical man" must be discredited at all costs, whether as disease and deterioration of mankind, or as his own hell and self-torture? And why? In favour of the "temperate zones"? In favour of the temperate men? The "moral"? The mediocre?—This for the chapter: "Morals as Timidity." . . .

In contrast to *laisser-aller,* every system of morals is a sort of tyranny against "nature" and also against "reason"; that is, however, no objection, unless one should again decree by some system of morals, that all kinds of tyranny and unreasonableness are unlawful. What is essential and invaluable in every system of morals, is that it is a long constraint. In order to understand Stocism, or Port-Royal, or Puritanism, one should remember the constraint under which every language has attained to strength and freedom —the metrical constraint, the tyranny of rhyme and rhythm. How much trouble have the poets and orators of every nation given themselves!—not excepting some of the prose writers of today, in whose ear dwells an inexorable conscientiousness—"for the sake of a folly," as utilitarian bunglers say, and thereby deem themselves wise—"from submission to arbitrary laws," as the anarchists say, and thereby fancy themselves "free," even free-spirited. The singular fact remains, however, that everything of the nature of freedom, elegance, boldness, dance, and masterly certainty, which exists or has existed, whether it be in thought itself, or in administration, or in speaking and persuading, in art just as in conduct, has only developed by means of the tyranny of such arbitrary law; and in all seriousness, it is not at all improbable that precisely this is "nature" and "natural"—and *not laisser-aller!* Every artist knows how different from the state of letting himself go, is his "most natural" condition, the free arranging, locating, disposing, and constructing in the moments of "inspiration"—and how strictly and delicately he then obeys a thousand laws, which, by their very rigidness and precision, defy all formulation by means of ideas (even the most stable idea has, in comparison therewith, something floating, manifold, and ambiguous in it). The essential thing "in heaven and in earth" is, apparently (to repeat it once more), that there should be long *obedience* in the same direction; there thereby results, and has always resulted in the long run, something which has made life worth living; for instance, virtue, art, music, dancing, reason, spirituality—anything whatever that is transfiguring, refined, foolish, or divine. The long bondage of the spirit, the distrustful constraint in the communicability of ideas, the discipline which the thinker imposed on himself to think in accordance with the rules of a church or a court, or conformable to Aristotelian premises, the persistent spiritual will to interpret everything that happened according to a Christian scheme, and in every occurrence to rediscover and justify the Christian God:—all this violence, arbitrariness, severity, dreadfulnesss, and unreasonableness, has proved itself the disciplinary means whereby the European spirit has attained its strength, its remorseless curiosity and subtle mobility; granted also that much irrecoverable strength and spirit had to be stifled, suffocated, and spoiled in the process (for here, as everywhere, "nature" shows herself as she is, in all her extravagant and *indifferent* magnificence, which is shocking, but nevertheless noble.) . . .

Whether it be hedonism,[1] pessimism, utilitarianism, or eudæmonism,[2] all those modes of thinking which measure the worth of things according to *pleasure* and *pain*, that is, according to accompanying circumstances and secondary considerations, are plausible modes of thought and naivetés, which every one conscious of *creative* powers and an artist's conscience will look down upon with scorn, though not without sympathy. Sympathy for *you!*—to be sure, that is not sympathy as you understand it: it is not sympathy for social "distress," for "society" with its sick and misfortuned, for the hereditarily vicious and defective who lie on the ground around us; still less is it sympathy for the grumbling, vexed,

[1] The view according to which pleasure is the good.—Ed.
[2] The view according to which happiness is the good.—Ed.

revolutionary slave-classes who strive after power—they call it "freedom." *Our* sympathy is a loftier and further-sighted sympathy: —we see how *man* dwarfs himself, how *you* dwarf him! and there are moments when we view *your* sympathy with an indescribable anguish, when we resist it,—when we regard your seriousness as more dangerous than any kind of levity. You want, if possible— and there is not a more foolish "if possible"—*to do away with suffering;* and we?—it really seems that *we* would rather have it increased and made worse than it has ever been! Well-being, as you understand it—is certainly not a goal; it seems to us an *end;* a condition which at once renders man ludicrous and contemptible —and makes his destruction *desirable!* The discipline of suffering, of *great* suffering—know ye not that it is only *this* discipline that has produced all the elevations of humanity hitherto? The tension of soul in misfortune which communicates to it its energy, its shuddering in view of rack and ruin, its inventiveness and bravery in undergoing, enduring, interpreting, and exploiting misfortune, and whatever depth, mystery, disguise, spirit, artifice, or greatness has been bestowed upon the soul—has it not been bestowed through suffering, through the discipline of great suffering? . . .

We Immoralists.—This world with which *we* are concerned, in which *we* have to fear and love, this almost invisible, inaudible world of delicate command and delicate obedience, a world of "almost" in every respect, captious, insidious, sharp, and tender— yes, it is well protected from clumsy spectators and familiar curiosity! We are woven into a strong net and garment of duties, and *cannot* disengage ourselves—precisely here, we are "men of duty," even we! Occasionally it is true we dance in our "chains" and betwixt our "swords"; it is none the less true that more often we gnash our teeth under the circumstances, and are impatient at the secret hardship of our lot. But do what we will, fools and appearances say of us: "These are men *without* duty,"—we have always fools and appearances against us!

Honesty, granting that it is the virtue from which we cannot rid ourselves, we free spirit—well, we will labour at it with all our perversity and love, and not tire of "perfecting" ourselves in *our* virtue, which alone remains: may its glance some day overspread like a gilded, blue, mocking twilight this aging civilisation with its dull gloomy seriousness! And if, nevertheless, our honesty should one day grow weary, and sigh, and stretch its limbs, and find us too hard, and would fain have it pleasanter, easier, and gentler, like an agreeable vice, let us remain *hard*, we latest Stoics, and let us send to its help whatever devilry we have in us:—our disgust at the clumsy and undefined, . . . our love of adventure, our sharpened and fastidious curiosity, our most subtle, disguised, intellectual Will to Power and universal conquest, which rambles and roves avidly around all the realms of the future—let us go with all our "devils" to the help of our "God"! It is probable that people will misunderstand and mistake us on that account: what does it matter!

PART II

Why Men Find It Natural to Do What Is Right

PLATO

The Virtues in the Individual [1]

The virtues in the state were the qualities of the citizen, as such, considered as playing the special part in society for which he was qualified by the predominance in his nature of the philosophic, the pugnacious, or the commercial spirit. But all three elements exist in every individual, who is thus a replica of society in miniature. In the perfect man reason will rule, with the spirited element as its auxiliary, over the bodily appetites. Self-control or temperance will be a condition of internal harmony, all the parts being content with their legitimate satisfactions. Justice finally appears, no longer only as a matter of external behaviour towards others, but as an internal order of the soul, from which right behaviour will necessarily follow. Injustice is the opposite state of internal discord and faction. To ask whether justice or injustice pays the better is now seen to be as absurd as to ask whether health is preferable to disease.[2]

And so, after a stormy passage, we have reached the land. We are fairly agreed that the same three elements exist alike in the state and in the individual soul.

From *The Republic of Plato*, trans. F. M. Cornford (Oxford: Clarendon Press, 1951), Bk. IV, pp. 139–143. Used by permission of the Clarendon Press, Oxford.

[1] As part of his attempt to refute the Sophistic doctrine set forth in the Myth of Gyges (see above, p. 25), Socrates works out a sort of blueprint of what he regards as the ideal state.—Ed.

[2] Translator's note.—Ed.

That is so.

Does it not follow at once that state and individual will be wise or brave by virtue of the same element in each and in the same way? Both will possess in the same manner any quality that makes for excellence.

That must be true.

Then it applies to justice: we shall conclude that a man is just in the same way that a state was just. And we have surely not forgotten that justice in the state meant that each of the three orders in it was doing its own proper work. So we may henceforth bear in mind that each one of us likewise will be a just person, fulfilling his proper function, only if the several parts of our nature fulfil theirs.

Certainly.

And it will be the business of reason to rule with wisdom and forethought on behalf of the entire soul; while the spirited element ought to act as its subordinate and ally. The two will be brought into accord, as we said earlier, by that combination of mental and bodily training which will tune up one string of the instrument and relax the other, nourishing the reasoning part of the study of noble literature and allaying the other's wildness by harmony and rhythm. When both have been thus nurtured and trained to know their own true functions, they must be set in command over the appetites, which form the greater part of each man's soul and are by nature insatiably covetous. They must keep watch lest this part, by battening on the pleasures that are called bodily, should grow so great and powerful that it will no longer keep to its own work, but will try to enslave the others and usurp a dominion to which it has no right, thus turning the whole of life upside down. At the same time, those two together will be the best of guardians for the entire soul and for the body against all enemies from without: the one will take counsel, while the other will do battle, following its ruler's commands and by its own bravery giving effect to the ruler's designs.

Yes, that is all true.

And so we call an individual brave in virtue of this spirited part of his nature, when, in spite of pain or pleasure, it holds fast to the injunctions of reason about what he ought or ought not to be afraid of.

True.

And wise in virtue of that small part which rules and issues these injunctions, possessing as it does the knowledge of what is good for each of the three elements and for all of them in common.

Certainly.

And, again, temperate by reason of the unanimity and concord of all three, when there is no internal conflict between the ruling element and its two subjects, but all are agreed that reason should be ruler.

Yes, that is an exact account of temperance, whether in the state or in the individual.

Finally, a man will be just by observing the principle we have so often stated.

Necessarily.

Now is there any indistinctness in our vision of justice, that might make it seem somehow different from what we found it to be in the state?

I don't think so.

Because, if we have any lingering doubt, we might make sure by comparing it with some commonplace notions. Suppose, for instance, that a sum of money were entrusted to our state or to an individual of corresponding character and training, would anyone imagine that such a person would be specially likely to embezzle it?

No.

And would he not be incapable of sacrilege and theft, or of treachery to friend or country; never false to an oath or any other compact; the last to be guilty of adultery or of neglecting parents or the due service of the gods?

Yes.

And the reason for all this is that each part of his nature is exercising its proper function, of ruling or of being ruled.

Yes, exactly.

Are you satisfied, then, that justice is the power which produces states or individuals of whom that is true, or must we look further?

There is no need; I am quite satisfied.

And so our dream has come true—I mean the inkling we had that, by some happy chance, we had lighted upon a rudimentary form of justice from the very moment when we set about founding our commonwealth. Our principle that the born shoemaker or carpenter had better stick to his trade turns out to have been an adumbration of justice; and that is why it has helped us. But in reality justice, though evidently analogous to this principle, is not a matter of external behaviour, but of the inward self and of attending to all that is, in the fullest sense, a man's proper concern. The just man does not allow the several elements in his soul to usurp one another's functions; he is indeed one who sets his house in order, by self-mastery and discipline coming to be at peace with himself, and bringing into tune those three parts, like the terms in the proportion of a musical scale, the highest and lowest notes and the mean between them, with all the intermediate intervals. Only when he has linked these parts together in a well-tempered harmony and has made himself one man instead of many, will he be ready to go about whatever he may have to do, whether it be making money and satisfying bodily wants, or business transactions, or the affairs of state. In all these fields when he speaks of just and honourable conduct, he will mean the behaviour that helps to produce and to preserve this habit of mind; and by wisdom he will mean the knowledge which presides over such conduct. Any action which tends to break down this habit will be for him unjust; and the notions governing it he will call ignorance and folly.

That is perfectly true, Socrates.

Good, said I. I believe we should not be thought altogether mistaken, if we claimed to have discovered the just man and the just state, and wherein their justice consists.

Indeed we should not.

Shall we make that claim, then?

Yes, we will.

So be it, said I. Next, I suppose, we have to consider injustice.

Evidently.

This must surely be a sort of civil strife among the three elements, whereby they usurp and encroach upon one another's functions and some one part of the soul rises up in rebellion against the whole, claiming a supremacy to which it has no right because its nature fits it only to be the servant of the ruling principle. Such turmoil and aberration we shall, I think, identify with injustice, intemperance, cowardice, ignorance, and in a word with all wickedness.

Exactly.

And now that we know the nature of justice and injustice, we can be equally clear about what is meant by acting justly and again by unjust action and wrongdoing.

How do you mean?

Plainly, they are exactly analogous to those wholesome and

The Virtues in the Individual / 61

unwholesome activities which respectively produce a healthy or unhealthy condition in the body; in the same way just and unjust conduct produce a just or unjust character. Justice is produced in the soul, like health in the body, by establishing the elements concerned in their natural relations of control and subordination, whereas injustice is like disease and means that this natural order is inverted.

Quite so.

It appears, then, that virtue is as it were the health and comeliness and well-being of the soul, as wickedness is desease, deformity, and weakness.

True.

And also that virtue and wickedness are brought about by one's way of life, honourable or disgraceful.

That follows.

So now it only remains to consider which is the more profitable course: to do right and live honourably and be just, whether or not anyone knows what manner of man you are, or to do wrong and be unjust, provided that you can escape the chastisement which might make you a better man.

But really, Socrates, it seems to me ridiculous to ask that question now that the nature of justice and injustice has been brought to light. People think that all the luxury and wealth and power in the world cannot make life worth living when the bodily constitution is going to rack and ruin; and are we to believe that, when the very principle whereby we live is deranged and corrupted, life will be worth living so long as a man can do as he will, and wills to do anything rather than to free himself from vice and wrong-doing and to win justice and virtue?

Yes, I replied, it is a ridiculous question.

JEAN-JACQUES ROUSSEAU

The Natural Man

Jean-Jacques Rousseau was born in Geneva in 1712, the son of a watchmaker who was also a dancing master. Raised as an orthodox Calvinist by an aunt, following his mother's early death, Rousseau left school at twelve and, after serving four years as an unwilling apprentice to various trades, fled Geneva for Savoy. For the next fifteen years, after being converted to Catholicism, he led an often-precarious existence, subsisting on odd jobs and the aid of friends. In 1743, with the help of a grande dame, *the French ambassador to Venice hired Rousseau as his secretary. His salary unpaid, Rousseau returned to Paris two years later and moved in with a servant girl who bore him five children and remained with him the rest of his life. In 1754, with the publication of* Discourse on Inequality, *Rousseau returned to Geneva, was reconverted to Calvinism, and entered into a long series of public controversies with fellow citizen Voltaire.* Émile *(1762) and* The Social Contract *(1762) condemned Rousseau to the life of a man persecuted by both Protestant and Catholic officialdom. His books were burned in Geneva and he was forced to flee France for England in 1765. Poverty-stricken and insane, Rousseau died in France in 1778.*

Let us lay it down as an incontrovertible rule that the first impulses of nature are always right; there is no original sin in the human heart, the how and why of the entrance of every vice can be traced. The only natural passion is self-love or selfishness taken in a wider sense. This selfishness is good in itself and in relation to ourselves; and as the child has no necessary relations to other people he is naturally indifferent to them; his self-love only becomes good or bad by the use made of it and the relations established by its means. Until the time is ripe for the appearance of reason, that guide of selfishness, the main thing is that the child shall do nothing because you are watching him or listening to him; in a word, nothing because of other people, but only what nature asks of him; then he will never do wrong.

I do not mean to say that he will never do any mischief, never

From the book Émile by Jean-Jacques Rousseau, trans. Barbara Foxley, pp. 56–57, 250–252, 252–254. Everyman's Library. Reprinted by permission of E. P. Dutton & Co., Inc., and J. M. Dent & Sons Ltd, London.

hurt himself, never break a costly ornament if you leave it within his reach. He might do much damage without doing wrong, since wrong-doing depends on the harmful intention which will never be his. If once he meant to do harm, his whole education would be ruined; he would be almost hopelessly bad. . . .

The morality of our actions consists entirely in the judgments we ourselves form with regard to them. If good is good, it must be good in the depth of our heart as well as in our actions; and the first reward of justice is the consciousness that we are acting justly. If moral goodness is in accordance with our nature, man can only be healthy in mind and body when he is good. If it is not so, and if man is by nature evil, he cannot cease to be evil without corrupting his nature, and goodness in him is a crime against nature. If he is made to do harm to his fellow-creatures, as the wolf is made to devour his prey, a humane man would be as depraved a creature as a pitiful wolf; and virtue alone would cause remorse.

My young friend, let us look within, let us set aside all personal prejudices and see whither our inclinations lead us. Do we take more pleasure in the sight of the sufferings of others or their joys? Is it pleasanter to do a kind action or an unkind action, and which leaves the more delightful memory behind it? Why do you enjoy the theatre? Do you delight in the crimes you behold? Do you weep over the punishment which overtakes the criminal? They say we are indifferent to everything but self-interest; yet we find our consolation in our sufferings in the charms of friendship and humanity, and even in our pleasures we should be too lonely and miserable if we had no one to share them with us. If there is no such thing as morality in man's heart, what is the source of his rapturous admiration of noble deeds, his passionate devotion to great men? What connection is there between self-interest and this enthusiasm for virtue? Why should I choose to be Cato dying by his own hand, rather than Caesar in his triumphs? Take from our hearts this love of what is noble and you rob us of the joy of life. The mean-spirited man in whom these delicious feelings have been stifled among vile passions, who by thinking of no one but himself comes at last to love no one but himself, this man feels no raptures, his cold heart no longer throbs with joy, and his eyes no longer fill with the sweet tears of sympathy, he delights in nothing; the wretch has neither life nor feeling, he is already dead.

There are many bad men in this world, but there are few of these dead souls, alive only to self-interest, and insensible to all that is right and good. We only delight in injustice so long as it is to our own advantage; in every other case we wish the innocent to be protected. If we see some act of violence or injustice in town or country, our hearts are at once stirred to their depths by an instinctive anger and wrath, which bids us go to the help of the oppressed; but we are restrained by a stronger duty, and the law deprives us of our right to protect the innocent. On the other hand, if some deed of mercy or generosity meets our eye, what reverence and love does it inspire! Do we not say to ourselves, "I should like to have done that myself"? What does it matter to us that two thousand years ago a man was just or unjust? and yet we take the same interest in ancient history as if it happened yesterday. What are the crimes of Cataline to me? I shall not be his victim. Why then have I the same horror of his crimes as if he were living now? We do not hate the wicked merely because of the harm they do to ourselves, but because they are wicked. Not only do we wish to be happy ourselves, we wish others to be happy too, and if this happiness does not interfere with our own happiness, it increases it. In conclusion, whether we will or not, we pity the unfortunate; when we see their suffering we suffer too. Even the most depraved are not wholly without this instinct, and it often leads them to self-contradiction. The highwayman who robs the traveller, clothes the nakedness of the poor; the fiercest murderer supports a fainting man.

Men speak of the voice of remorse, the secret punishment of hidden crimes, by which such are often brought to light. Alas! who does not know its unwelcome voice? We speak from experience, and we would gladly stifle this imperious feeling which causes us such agony. Let us obey the call of nature; we shall see that her yoke is easy and that when we give heed to her voice we find a joy in the answer of a good conscience. The wicked fears and flees from her; he delights to escape from himself; his anxious eyes look around him for some object of diversion; without bitter satire and rude mockery he would always be sorrowful; the scornful laugh is his one pleasure. Not so the just man, who find his peace within himself; there is joy not malice in his laughter, a joy which springs from his own heart; he is as cheerful alone as in company, his satisfaction does not depend on those who approach him; it includes them.

Cast your eyes over every nation of the world; peruse every

volume of its history; in the midst of all these strange and cruel forms of worship, among this amazing variety of manners and customs, you will everywhere find the same ideas of right and justice; everywhere the same principles of morality, the same ideas of good and evil. The old paganism gave birth to abominable gods who would have been punished as scoundrels here below, gods who merely offered, as a picture of supreme happiness, crimes to be committed and lust to be gratified. But in vain did vice descend from the abode of the gods armed with their sacred authority; the moral instinct refused to admit it into the heart of man. While the debaucheries of Jupiter were celebrated, the continence of Xenocrates was revered; the chaste Lucrece adored the shameless Venus, the bold Roman offered sacrifices to Fear; he invoked the god who mutilated his father, and he died without a murmur at the hand of his own father. The most unworthy gods were worshipped by the noblest men. The sacred voice of nature was stronger than the voice of the gods, and won reverence upon earth; it seemed to relegate guilt and the guilty alike to heaven.

There is . . . at the bottom of our hearts an innate principle of justice and virtue, by which, in spite of our maxims, we judge our own actions or those of others to be good or evil; and it is this principle that I call conscience. . . .

Self-interest, so they say, induces each of us to agree for the common good. But how is it that the good man consents to this to his own hurt? Does a man go to death from self-interest? No doubt each man acts for his own good, but if there is no such thing as moral good to be taken into consideration, self-interest will only enable you to account for the deeds of the wicked; possibly you will not attempt to do more. A philosophy which could find no place for good deeds would be too detestable; you would find yourself compelled either to find some mean purpose, some wicked motive, or to abuse Socrates and slander Regulus. If such doctrines ever took root among us, the voice of nature, together with the voice of reason, would constantly protest against them, till no adherent of such teaching could plead an honest excuse for his partisanship.

It is no part of my scheme to enter at present into metaphysical discussions which neither you nor I can understand, discussions which really lead nowhere. I have told you already that I do not wish to philosophise with you, but to help you to consult your own heart. If all the philosophers in the world should prove that I am wrong, and you feel that I am right, that is all I ask.

For this purpose it is enough to lead you to distinguish between our acquired ideas and our natural feelings; for feeling precedes knowledge; and since we do not learn to seek what is good for us and avoid what is bad for us, but get this desire from nature, in the same way the love of good and the hatred of evil are as natural to us as our self-love. The decrees of conscience are not judgments but feelings. Although all our ideas come from without, the feelings by which they are weighed are within us, and it is by these feelings alone that we perceive fitness or unfitness of things in relation to ourselves, which leads us to seek or shun these things.

To exist is to feel; our feeling is undoubtedly earlier than our intelligence, and we had feelings before we had ideas.[1] Whatever may be the cause of our being, it has provided for our preservation by giving us feelings suited to our nature; and no one can deny that these at least are innate. These feelings, so far as the individual is concerned, are self-love, fear, pain, the dread of death, the desire for comfort. Again, if, as it is impossible to doubt, man is by nature sociable, or at least fitted to become sociable, he can only be so by means of other innate feelings, relative to his kind; for if only physical well-being were considered, men would certainly be scattered rather than brought together. But the motive power of conscience is derived from the moral system formed through this twofold relation to himself and to his fellow-men. To know good is not to love it; this knowledge is not innate in man; but as soon as his reason leads him to perceive it, his conscience impels him to love it; it is this feeling which is innate.

So I do not think, my young friend, that it is impossible to explain the immediate force of conscience as a result of our own nature, independent of reason itself. And even should it be impossible, it is unnecessary; for those who deny this principle, admitted and received by everybody else in the world, do not

[1] In some respects ideas are feelings and feelings are ideas. Both terms are appropriate to any perception with which we are concerned, appropriate both to the object of that perception and to ourselves who are affected by it; it is merely the order in which we are affected which decides the appropriate term. When we are chiefly concerned with the object and only think of ourselves as it were by reflection, that is an idea; when, on the other hand, the impression received excites our chief attention and we only think in the second place of the object which caused it, it is a feeling.

prove that there is no such thing; they are content to affirm, and when we affirm its existence we have quite as good grounds as they, while we have moreover the witness within us, the voice of conscience, which speaks on its own behalf. If the first beams of judgment dazzle us and confuse the objects we behold, let us wait till our feeble sight grows clear and strong, and in the light of reason we shall soon behold these very objects as nature has already showed them to us. Or rather let us be simpler and less pretentious; let us be content with the first feelings we experience in ourselves, since science always brings us back to these, unless it has led us astray.

Conscience! Conscience! Divine instinct, immortal voice from heaven; sure guide for a creature ignorant and finite indeed; yet intelligent and free; infallible judge of good and evil, making man like to God! In thee consists the excellence of man's nature and the morality of his actions; apart from thee, I find nothing in myself to raise me above the beasts—nothing but the sad privilege of wandering from one error to another, by the help of an unbridled understanding and a reason which knows no principle.

SHAFTESBURY

Virtue and the Natural Affections

Anthony Ashley Cooper, third Earl of Shaftesbury, was born in London in 1671 and brought up by his grandfather in the teachings of the English philosopher Locke. He traveled abroad from 1686 to 1689, and upon returning to England was elected a Whig member of Parliament. Ill health forced him to retire after four years. While Shaftesbury was in Holland, an imperfect edition of the Enquiry Concerning Virtue or Merit *was published. Because of his active participation in the general elections of 1700 and 1701, William III offered him the position of secretary of state, a position he was unable to accept. After William's death, Shaftesbury left England for Holland but returned in 1704 to devote himself to literary pursuits. He married two years before his death in 1713.*

Our business . . . will be to prove:

I. That to have the natural, kindly, or generous affections strong and powerful towards the good of the public is to have the chief means and power of self-enjoyment. And that to want them is certain misery and ill.
II. That to have the private or self-affections too strong, or beyond their degree of subordinacy to the kindly and natural, is also miserable.
III. And, that to have the unnatural affections (viz. such as are neither founded on the interest of the kind, or public, nor of the private person, or creature himself) is to be miserable in the highest degree.

To begin therefore with this proof: That to have the natural affections (such as are founded in love, complacency, good will, and in a sympathy with the kind or species) is to have the chief means and power of self-enjoyment; and that to want them is certain misery and ill.

We may inquire, first, what those are which we call pleasures or satisfactions, from whence happiness is generally computed. They are (according to the common distinction) satisfactions and pleasures either of the body or of the mind.

From the Earl of Shaftesbury, *An Inquiry Concerning Virtue,* Bk. II, pp. 33–36, 46–48, 60–61; reprinted in *British Moralists,* ed. L. A. Selby-Bigge (Oxford, 1897), Vol. I. Occasional changes in spelling and punctuation have been made.

That the latter of these satisfactions are the greatest is allowed by most people and may be proved by this: That whenever the mind, having conceived a high opinion of the worth of any action or behavior, has received the strongest impression of this sort and is wrought up to the highest pitch or degree of passion towards the subject; at such time it sets itself above all bodily pain as well as pleasure and can be noway diverted from its purpose by flattery or terror of any kind. Thus we see Indians, barbarians, malefactors and even the most execrable villains, for the sake of a particular gang or society or through some cherished notion or principle of honor or gallantry, revenge, or gratitude, embrace any manner of hardship and defy torments and death. . . .

Now the mental enjoyments are either actually the very natural affections themselves in their immediate operation; or they wholly in a manner proceed from them and are no other than their effects.

If so, it follows that the natural affections duly established in a rational creature, being the only means which can procure him a constant series or succession of the mental enjoyments, they are the only means which can procure him a certain and solid happiness.

Now, in the first place, to explain how much the natural affections are in themselves the highest pleasures and enjoyments: there should, methinks, be little need of proving this to anyone of human kind who has ever known the condition of the mind under a lively affection of love, gratitude, bounty, generosity, pity, succor, or whatever else is of a social or friendly sort. He who has ever so little knowledge of human nature is sensible what pleasure the mind perceives when it is touched in this generous way. The difference we find between solitude and company, between a common company and that of friends, the reference of almost all our pleasures to mutual converse, and the dependence they have on society either present or imagined; all these are sufficient proofs in our behalf.

How much the social pleasures are superior to any other may be known by visible tokens and effects. The very outward features, the marks and signs which attend this sort of joy, are expressive of a more intense, clear, and undisturbed pleasure than those which attend the satisfaction of thirst, hunger, and other ardent appetites. But more particularly still may this superiority be known from the actual prevalence and ascendency of this sort of affection over all besides. Wherever it presents itself with any advantage, it silences and appeases every other motion of pleasure. No joy merely of sense can be a match for it. . . .

There are two things which to a rational creature must be horridly offensive and grievous: viz. to have the reflection in his mind of any unjust action or behavior which he knows to be naturally odious and ill-deserving, or of any foolish action or behavior which he knows to be prejudicial to his own interest or happiness.

The former of these is alone properly called conscience, whether in a moral or religious sense. For to have awe and terror of the Deity does not, of itself, imply conscience. No one is esteemed the more conscientious for the fear of evil spirits, conjurations, enchantments, or whatever may proceed from any unjust, capricious, or devilish nature. Now to fear God any otherwise than as in consequence of some justly blameable and imputable act is to fear a devilish nature, not a divine one. Nor does the fear of hell, or a thousand terrors of the Deity, imply conscience, unless where there is an apprehension of what is wrong, odious, morally deformed and ill-deserving. And where this is the case, there conscience must have effect, and punishment of necessity be apprehended, even though it be not expressly threatened. . . .

It has already been said that no creature can maliciously and intentionally do ill without being sensible, at the same time, that he deserves ill. And in this respect, every sensible creature may be said to have conscience. For with all mankind and all intelligent creatures this must ever hold: That *what* they know they deserve from everyone, *that* they necessarily must fear and expect from all. And thus suspicions and ill apprehensions must arise, with terror both of men and of the Deity. But besides this, there must in every rational creature be yet farther conscience: viz. from a sense of deformity in what is thus ill-deserving and unnatural; and from a consequent shame or regret of incurring what is odious and moves aversion.

There scarcely is or can be any creature whom, consciousness of villainy, as such merely, does not at all offend, nor anything opprobrious or heinously imputable move or affect. If there be such a one, it is evident he must be absolutely indifferent towards moral good or ill. If this ideed be his case, it will be allowed he can be noway capable of natural affection. If not of that, then neither of any social pleasure or mental enjoyment, as shown above; but on the contrary, he must be subject to all manner of horrid, unnatural, and ill affection. So that to want conscience, or natural sense of the odiousness of crime and injustice, is to be most of all miserable in life. But where conscience or sense of this sort remains, there, consequently, whatever is committed against it must of necessity, by means of reflection, as we have shown, be continually shameful, grievous and offensive.

A man who in a passion happens to kill his companion relents immediately on the sight of what he has done. His revenge is changed into pity, and his hatred turned against himself—and this merely by the power of the object. On this account he suffers agonies; the subject of this continually occurs to him; and of this he has a constant ill remembrance and displeasing consciousness. If on the other side, we suppose him not to relent or suffer any real concern or shame, then, either he has no sense of the deformity of the crime and injustice, no natural affection, and consequently no happiness or peace within; or if he has any sense of moral worth or goodness, it must be of a perplexed and contradictory kind. He must pursue an inconsistent notion, idolize some false species of virtue, and affect as noble, gallant or worthy that which is irrational and absurd. . . . For it is impossible that a cruel enthusiast or bigot, a persecutor, a murderer, a bravo, a pirate, or any villain of less degree, who is false to the society of mankind in general and contradicts natural affection, should have any fixed principle at all, any real standard or measure by which he can regulate his esteem, or any solid reason by which to form his approbation of any one moral act. And thus the more he sets up honor or advances zeal, the worse he renders his nature and the more detestable his character. The more he engages in the love or admiration of any action or practice as great and glorious, which is in itself morally ill and vicious, the more contradiction and self-disapprobation he must incur. For there being nothing more certain than this: That no natural affection can be contradicted, nor any unnatural one advanced without a prejudice in some degree to call natural affection in general; it must follow that inward deformity growing greater by the encouragement of unnatural affection, there must be so much the more subject for dissatisfactory reflection the more any false principle of honor, any false religion, or superstition prevails. . . .

Treachery and ingratitude are in strictness mere negative vices and, in themselves, no real passions, having neither aversion or inclination belonging to them, but are derived from the defect, unsoundness, or corruption of the affections in general. But when these vices become remarkable in a character and arise in a manner from inclination and choice; when they are so forward and active as to appear of their own accord, without any pressing occasion, it is apparent they borrow something of the mere unnatural passions and are derived from malice, envy, and inveteracy, as explained above.

It may be objected here, that these passions, unnatural as they are, carry still a sort of pleasure with them; and that however barbarous a pleasure it be, yet still it is a pleasure and satisfaction which is found in pride, or tyranny, revenge, malice, or cruelty exerted. Now if it be possible in nature that anyone can feel a barbarous or malicious joy otherwise than in consequence of mere anguish and torment, then may we perhaps allow this kind of satisfaction to be called pleasure or delight. But the case is evidently contrary. To love and to be kind, to have social or natural affection, complacency and good will, is to feel immediate satisfaction and genuine content. It is in itself original joy, depending on no preceding pain or uneasiness and producing nothing beside satisfaction merely. On the other side, animosity, hatred, and bitterness is original misery and torment, producing no other pleasure or satisfaction than as the unnatural desire is for the instant satisfied by something which appeases it. How strong soever this pleasure, therefore, may appear, it only the more implies the misery of that state which produces it. For as the cruelest bodily pains do by intervals of assuagement produce (as has been shown) the highest bodily pleasure, so the fiercest and most raging torments of the mind do, by certain moments of relief, afford the greatest of mental enjoyments to those who know little of the truer kind.

The men of gentlest dispositions and best of tempers have at some time or other been sufficiently acquainted with those disturbances, which, at ill hours, even small occasions are apt to raise. From these slender experiences of harshness and ill humor, they fully know and will confess the ill moments which are passed when the temper is ever so little galled or fretted. How must it fare, therefore, with those who hardly know any better hours in life and who, for the greatest part of it, are agitated by a through active spleen, a close and settled malignity and rancor? How lively must be the sense of every thwarting and controlling accident? How great must be the shocks of disappointment, the stings of affront, and the agonies of a working antipathy against the multiplied objects of offence. Nor can it be wondered at, if to persons thus agitated and oppressed, it seems a high delight to appease and allay for the while those furious and rough motions by an indulgence of their passion in mischief and revenge.

Now as to the consequences of this unnatural state in respect of interest and the common circumstances of life, upon what terms a person, who has in this manner lost all which we call nature, can be supposed to stand, in respect of the society of mankind; how he feels himself in it; what sense he has of his own disposition towards others and of the mutual disposition of others towards himself; this is easily conceived.

What enjoyment or rest is there for one who is not conscious of the merited affection or love but, on the contrary, of the ill will and hatred of every human soul? What ground must this afford for horror and despair? What foundation of fear and continual apprehension from mankind and from superior powers? How thorough and deep must be that melancholy, which being once moved, has nothing soft or pleasing from the side of friendship to allay or divert it? Wherever such a creature turns himself, whichever way he casts his eye, everything around must appear ghastly and horrid; everything hostile and, as it were, bent against a private and single being, who is thus divided from everything and at defiance and war with the rest of nature.

It is thus, at last, that a mind becomes a wilderness, where all is laid waste, everything fair and goodly removed, and nothing extant beside what is savage and deformed. Now if banishment from one's country, removal to a foreign place, or anything which looks like solitude or desertion be so heavy to endure, what must it be to feel this inward banishment, this real estrangement from human commerce; and to be after this manner in a desert and in the horridest of solitudes, even when in the midst of society? What must it be to live in the disagreement with everything, this irreconcilableness and opposition to the order and government of the universe?

Hence it appears that the greatest of miseries accompanies that state which is consequent to the loss of natural affection; and that to have those horrid, monstrous, and unnatural affections is to be miserable in the highest degree.

JOHN STUART MILL

Utilitarianism [1]

John Stuart Mill was born in 1806. His father, James Mill, a disciple of Bentham, instructed him from an early age in classical languages and the principles of political economy. After a brief visit to the continent, Mill returned to London to read for the law at the age of fifteen. Two years later, he founded the Westminster Review *and entered the civil service as an employee of the East India Company, a position he retained for the rest of his professional life. Under the influence of Harriet Taylor, for many years his closest friend and eventually his wife, Mill tried to liberalize the doctrines of Benthamite utilitarianism. He served as a member of the House of Commons from 1865 to 1868. Among his major works are the following:* A System of Logic *(1843),* Principles of Political Economy *(1848),* On Liberty *(1859),* Considerations on Representative Government *(1861), and* Utilitarianism *(1863). He died in 1873.*

The question is often asked, and properly so, in regard to any supposed moral standard—What is its sanction? what are the motives to obey? or more specifically, what is the source of its obligation? whence does it derive its binding force? It is a necessary part of moral philosophy to provide the answer to this question, which, though frequently assuming the shape of an objection to the utilitarian morality, as if it had some special applicability to that above others, really arises in regard to all standards. It arises, in fact, whenever a person is called on to *adopt* a standard, or refer morality to any basis on which he has not been accustomed to rest it. For the customary morality, that which education and opinion have consecrated is the only one which presents itself to the mind with the feeling of being *in itself* obligatory; and when a person is asked to believe that this morality *derives* its

From John Stuart Mill, *Utilitarianism* (15th ed.), Chap. III (London, Longmans Green, 1907).

[1] In an earlier part of the essay, Mill characterizes utilitarian doctrine as follows: "The creed which accepts as the foundation of morals 'utility' or 'the greatest happiness principle' holds that actions are right in proportion as they tend to promote happiness; wrong as they tend to produce the reverse of happiness." In the following chapter he shows what "sanctions," that is, what incentives and reasons, there are for judging actions by the test of utility.—Ed.

obligation from some general principle round which custom has not thrown the same halo, the assertion is to him a paradox; the supposed corollaries seem to have a more binding force than the original theorem; the superstructure seems to stand better without than with what is represented as its foundation. He says to himself, I feel that I am bound not to rob or murder, betray or deceive; but why am I bound to promote the general happiness? If my own happiness lies in something else, why may I not give that the preference?

If the view adopted by the utilitarian philosophy of the nature of the moral sense be correct, this difficulty will always present itself until the influences which form moral character have taken the same hold of the principle which they have taken of some of the consequences—until, by the improvement of education, the feeling of unity with our fellow creatures shall be (what it cannot be denied that Christ intended it to be) as deeply rooted in our character, and to our own consciousness as completely a part of our nature, as the horror of crime is in an ordinarily well brought up young person. In the meantime, however, the difficulty has no peculiar application to the doctrine of utility, but is inherent in every attempt to analyze morality and reduce it to principles; which, unless the principle is already in men's minds invested with as much sacredness as any of its applications, always seems to divest them of a part of their sanctity.

The principle of utility either has, or there is no reason why it might not have, all the sanctions which belong to any other system of morals. Those sanctions are either external or internal. Of the external sanctions it is not necessary to speak at any length. They are the hope of favor and the fear of displeasure from our fellow creatures or from the Ruler of the Universe, along with whatever we may have of sympathy or affection for them, or of love and awe of Him, inclining us to do His will independently of selfish consequences. There is evidently no reason why all these motives for observance should not attach themselves to the utilitarian morality as completely and as powerfully as to any other. Indeed, those of them which refer to our fellow creatures are sure to do so, in proportion to the amount of general intelligence; for whether there be any other ground of moral obligation than the general happiness or not, men do desire happiness; and however imperfect may be their own practice, they desire and commend all conduct in others towards themselves by which they think their happiness is promoted. With regard to the religious motive, if men believe, as most profess to do, in the goodness of God, those who think that conduciveness to the general happiness is the essence or even only the criterion of good must necessarily believe that it is also that which God approves. The whole force therefore of external reward and punishment, whether physical or moral, and whether proceeding from God or from our fellow men, together with all that the capacities of human nature admit of disinterested devotion to either, become available to enforce the utilitarian morality, in proportion as that morality is recognized; and the more powerfully, the more the appliances of education and general cultivation are bent to the purpose.

So far as to external sanctions. The internal sanction of duty, whatever our standard of duty may be, is one and the same—a feeling in our own mind; a pain, more or less intense, attendant on violation of duty, which in properly cultivated moral natures rises, in the more serious cases, into shrinking from it as an impossibility. This feeling, when disinterested and connecting itself with the pure idea of duty, and not with some particular form of it, or with any of the merely accessory circumstances, is the essence of conscience; though in that complex phenomenon as it actually exists, the simple fact is in general all encrusted over with collateral associations derived from sympathy, from love, and still more from fear; from all the forms of religious feeling; from the recollections of childhood and of all our past life; from self-esteem, desire of the esteem of others, and occasionally even self-abasement. This extreme complication is, I apprehend, the origin of the sort of mystical character which, by a tendency of the human mind of which there are many other examples, is apt to be attributed to the idea of moral obligation, and which leads people to believe that the idea cannot possibly attach itself to any other objects than those which, by a supposed mysterious law, are found in our present experience to excite it. Its binding force, however, consists in the existence of a mass of feeling which must be broken through in order to do what violates our standard of right, and which, if we do nevertheless violate that standard, will probably have to be encountered afterwards in the form of remorse. Whatever theory we have of the nature or origin of conscience, this is what essentially constitutes it.

The ultimate sanction, therefore, of all morality (external motives apart) being a subjective feeling in our own minds, I see nothing embarrassing to those whose standard is utility in the question, what is the sanction of that particular standard? We may answer, the same as of all other moral standards—the conscientious feelings of mankind. Undoubtedly this sanction has no binding efficacy on those who do not possess the feelings it appeals to; but neither will these persons be more obedient to any other moral principle than to the utilitarian one. On them morality of any kind has no hold but through the external sanctions. Meanwhile the feelings exist, a fact in human nature, the reality of which, and the great power with which they are capable of acting on those in whom they have been duly cultivated, are proved by experience. No reason has ever been shown why they may not be cultivated to as great intensity in connection with the utilitarian, as with any other rule of morals.

There is, I am aware, a disposition to believe that a person [2] who sees in moral obligation a transcendental fact, an objective reality belonging to the province of 'things in themselves,' is likely to be more obedient to it than one who believes it to be entirely subjective, having its seat in human consciousness only. But whatever a person's opinion may be on this point of ontology, the force he is really urged by is his own subjective feeling, and is exactly measured by its strength. No one's belief that duty is an objective reality is stronger than the belief that God is so; yet the belief in God, apart from the expectation of actual reward and punishment, only operates on conduct through, and in proportion to, the subjective religious feeling. The sanction, so far as it is disinterested, is always in the mind itself; and the notion, therefore, of the transcendental moralists must be that this sanction will not exist *in* the mind unless it is believed to have its root out of the mind; and that if a person is able to say to himself, "This which is restraining me, and which is called my conscience, is only a feeling in my own mind," he may possibly draw the conclusion that when the feeling ceases the obligation ceases, and that if he find the feeling inconvenient, he may disregard it and endeavor to get rid of it. But is this danger confined to the utilitarian morality? Does the belief that moral obligation has its seat outside the mind make the feeling of it too strong to be got rid of? The fact is so far

[2] For example, Kant.—Ed.

otherwise that all moralists admit and lament the ease with which, in the generality of minds, conscience can be silenced or stifled. The question, "Need I obey my conscience?" is quite as often put to themselves by persons who never heard of the principle of utility, as by its adherents. Those whose conscientious feelings are so weak as to allow of their asking this question, if they answer it affirmatively, will not do so because they believe in the transcendental theory, but because of the external sanctions.

It is not necessary, for the present purpose, to decide whether the feeling of duty is innate or implanted. Assuming it to be innate, it is an open question to what objects it naturally attaches itself; for the philosophic supporters of that theory are now agreed that the intuitive perception is of principles of morality and not of the details. If there be anything innate in the matter, I see no reason why the feeling which is innate should not be that of regard to the pleasures and pains of others. If there is any principle of morals which is intuitively obligatory, I should say it must be that. If so, the intuitive ethics would coincide with the utilitarian, and there would be no further quarrel between them. Even as it is, the intuitive moralists, though they believe that there are other intuitive moral obligations, do already believe this to be one; for they unanimously hold that a large *portion* of morality turns upon the consideration due to the interests of our fellow creatures. Therefore, if the belief in the transcendental origin of moral obligation gives any additional efficacy to the internal sanction, it appears to me that the utilitarian principle has already the benefit of it.

On the other hand, if, as is my own belief, the moral feelings are not innate but acquired, they are not for that reason the less natural. It is natural to man to speak, to reason, to build cities, to cultivate the ground, though these are acquired faculties. The moral feelings are not indeed a part of our nature, in the sense of being in any perceptible degree present in all of us; but this, unhappily, is a fact admitted by those who believe the most strenuously in their transcendental origin. Like the other acquired capacities above referred to, the moral faculty, if not a part of our nature, is a natural outgrowth from it; capable, like them, in a certain, small degree, of springing up spontaneously; and susceptible of being brought by cultivation to a high degree of development. Unhappily it is also susceptible, by a sufficient use of the external sanctions and of the force of early impressions, of being cultivated in almost any direction, so that there is hardly anything so absurd or so mischievous that it may not, by means of these influences, be made to act on the human mind with all the authority of conscience. To doubt that the same potency might be given by the same means to the principle of utility, even if it had no foundation in human nature, would be flying in the face of all experience.

But moral associations which are wholly of artificial creation, when intellectual culture goes on, yield by degrees to the dissolving force of analysis; and if the feeling of duty, when associated with utility, would appear equally arbitrary; if there were no leading department of our nature, no powerful class of sentiments, with which that association would harmonize, which would make us feel it congenial and incline us not only to foster it in others (for which we have abundant interested motives), but also to cherish it in ourselves—if there were not, in short, a natural basis of sentiment for utilitarian morality, it might well happen that this association also, even after it had been implanted by education, might be analyzed away.

But there *is* this basis of powerful natural sentiment; and this it is which, when once the general happiness is recognized as the ethical standard, will constitute the strength of the utilitarian morality. This firm foundation is that of the social feelings of mankind; the desire to be in unity with our fellow creatures, which is already a powerful principle in human nature, and happily one of those which tend to become stronger, even without express inculcation, from the influences of advancing civilization. The social state is at once so natural, so necessary, and so habitual to man, that, except in some unusual circumstances or by an effort of voluntary abstraction, he never conceives himself otherwise than as a member of a body; and this association is riveted more and more, as mankind are further removed from the state of savage independence. Any condition, therefore, which is essential to a state of society, becomes more and more an inseparable part of every person's conception of the state of things which he is born into, and which is the destiny of a human being. Now society between human beings, except in the relation of master and slave, is manifestly impossible on any other footing than that the interests of all are to be consulted. Society between equals can only exist on the understanding that the interests of all are to be regarded equally. And since in all states of civilization, every person, except an absolute monarch, has equals, everyone is obliged to live on these terms with somebody; and in every age some advance is made towards a state in which it will be impossible to live permanently on other terms with anybody. In this way people grow up unable to conceive as possible to them a state of total disregard of other people's interests. They are under a necessity of conceiving themselves as at least abstaining from all the grosser injuries, and (if only for their own protection) living in a state of constant protest against them. They are also familiar with the fact of co-operating with others, and proposing to themselves a collective, not an individual, interest as the aim (at least for the time being) of their actions. So long as they are co-operating, their ends are identified with those of others; there is at least a temporary feeling that the interests of others are their own interests. Not only does all strengthening of social ties, and all healthy growth of society, give to each individual a stronger personal interest in practically consulting the welfare of others, it also leads him to identify his *feelings* more and more with their good, or at least with an even greater degree of practical consideration for it. He comes, as though instinctively, to be conscious of himself as a being who *of course* pays regard to others. The good of others becomes to him a thing naturally and necessarily to be attended to, like any of the physical conditions of our existence. Now, whatever amount of this feeling a person has, he is urged by the strongest motive both of interest and of sympathy to demonstrate it, and to the utmost of his power encourage it in others; and even if he has none of it himself, he is as greatly interested as any one else that others should have it. Consequently the smallest germs of the feeling are laid hold of and nourished by the contagion of sympathy and the influences of education; and a complete web of corroborative association is woven round it, by the powerful agency of the external sanctions. . . .

This feeling [viz., concern for the good of others] in most individuals is much inferior in strength to their selfish feelings, and is often wanting altogether. But to those who have it, it possesses all the characters of a natural feeling. It does not present itself to their minds as a superstition of education, or a law despotically imposed by the power of society, but as an attribute which it would not be well for them to be without. This conviction is the ultimate sanction of the greatest happiness morality. This it is which makes any mind of well-developed feelings work with, and not against, the outward motives to care for others, afforded by what I have called the external sanctions; and, when those sanctions are wanting, or act in an opposite direction, constitutes in itself a powerful internal binding force, in proportion to the sensitiveness and thoughtfulness of the character; since few but those whose mind is a moral blank could bear to lay out their course of life on the plan of paying no regard to others except so far as their own private interest compels.

PART III
Morality and Human Nature

JOHN DEWEY

Does Human Nature Change?

John Dewey, a leading pragmatist, was born in Vermont in 1859 and was educated there until his graduation from the state university twenty years later. After receiving his doctorate from Johns Hopkins University in 1884, Dewey taught at several universities, including Columbia and the University of Chicago, where he began teaching philosophy in 1894. There he founded a progressive school and began his voluminous writings on education (including The School and Society, *1899;* Experience and Education; *and* Education and Democracy) *which revolutionized much of the American educational system. Dewey's writings had an impact not only on education and philosophy (*Ethics, *1908;* How We Think, *1910;* Essays in Experimental Logic, *1916;* Reconstruction in Philosophy, *1920;* Logic, the Theory of Inquiry, *1939;* The Theory of Valuation, *1939), but also on social psychology (*Human Nature and Conduct, *1922) and politics (*The Public and Its Problems, *1927;* Individualism, Old and New, *1930;* Liberalism and Social Action, *1935). Dewey remained active as a professor emeritus from Columbia and in the 1930's attempted to create a People's Party, which would offer an alternative to conservative and totalitarian parties. He died in 1952 at the age of ninety-two.*

I have come to the conclusion that those who give different answers to the question I have asked in the title of this article are talking about different things. This statement in itself, however, is too easy a way out of the problem to be satisfactory. For there

From John Dewey, "Does Human Nature Change?" *The Rotarian,* February 1938. Reprinted by permission.

is a real problem, and so far as the question is a practical one instead of an academic one, I think the proper answer is that human nature *does* change.

By the practical side of the question, I mean the question whether or not important, almost fundamental, changes in the ways of human belief and action have taken place and are capable of still taking place. But to put this question in its proper perspective, we have first to recognize the sense in which human nature does not change. I do not think it can be shown that the innate needs of men have changed since man became man or that there is any evidence that they will change as long as man is on the earth.

By "needs" I mean the inherent demands that men make because of their constitution. Needs for food and drink and for moving about, for example, are so much a part of our being that we cannot imagine any condition under which they would cease to be. There are other things not so directly physical that seem to me equally engrained in human nature. I would mention as examples the need for some kind of companionship; the need for exhibiting energy, for bringing one's powers to bear upon surrounding conditions; the need for both cooperation with an emulation of one's fellows for mutual aid and combat alike; the need for some sort of aesthetic expression and satisfaction; the need to lead and to follow; etc.

Whether my particular examples are well chosen or not does not matter so much as does recognition of the fact that there are some tendencies so integral a part of human nature that the latter would not be human nature if they changed. These tendencies used to be called instincts. Psychologists are now more chary of using that word than they used to be. But the word by which the tendencies are called does not matter much in comparison to the fact that human nature has its own constitution.

Where we are likely to go wrong after the fact is recognized that there is something unchangeable in the structure of human nature is the inference we draw from it. We suppose that the manifestation of these needs is also unalterable. We suppose that the manifestations we have got used to are as natural and as unalterable as are the needs from which they spring.

The need for food is so imperative that we call the persons insane who persistently refuse to take nourishment. But what kinds of food are wanted and used is a matter of acquired habit influenced by both physical environment and social custom. To civilized people today, eating human flesh is an entirely unnatural thing. Yet there have been peoples to whom it seemed natural because it was socially authorized and even highly esteemed. There are well-accredited stories of persons, needing support from others, who have refused palatable and nourishing foods because they were not accustomed to them; the alien foods were so "unnatural" they preferred to starve rather than eat them.

Aristotle spoke for an entire social order as well as for himself when he said that slavery existed by nature. He would have regarded efforts to abolish slavery from society as an idle and utopian effort to change human nature where it was unchangeable. For according to him it was not simply the desire to be a master that was engrained in human nature. There were persons who were born with such an inherently slavish nature that it did violence to human nature to set them free.

The assertion that human nature cannot be changed is heard when social changes are urged as reforms and improvements of existing conditions. It is always heard when the proposed changes in institutions or conditions stand in sharp opposition to what exists. If the conservative were wiser, he would rest his objections in most cases, not upon the unchangeability of human nature, but upon the inertia of custom; upon the resistance that acquired habits offer to change after they are once acquired. It is hard to teach an old dog new tricks and it is harder yet to teach society to adopt customs which are contrary to those which have long prevailed. Conservatism of this type would be intelligent and it would compel those wanting change not only to moderate their pace, but also to ask how the changes they desire could be introduced with a minimum of shock and dislocation.

Nevertheless, there are few social changes that can be opposed on the ground that they are contrary to human nature itself. A proposal to have a society get along without food and drink is one of the few that are of this kind. Proposals to form communities in which there is no cohabitation have been made and the communities have endured for a time. But they are so nearly contrary to human nature that they have not endured long. These cases are almost the only ones in which social change can be opposed simply on the ground that human nature cannot be changed.

Take the institution of war, one of the oldest, most socially reputable of all human institutions. Efforts for stable peace are often opposed on the ground that man is by nature a fighting animal and that this phase of his nature is unalterable. The failure of peace movements in the past can be cited in support of this view. In fact, however, war is as much a social pattern as is the domestic slavery which the ancients thought to be an immutable fact.

I have already said that, in my opinion, combativeness is a constituent part of human nature. But I have also said that the manifestations of these native elements are subject to change because they are affected by custom and tradition. War does not exist because man has combative instincts, but because social conditions and forces have led, almost forced, these "instincts" into this channel.

There are a large number of other channels in which the need for combat has been satisfied, and there are other channels not yet discovered or explored into which it could be led with equal satisfaction. There is war against disease, against poverty, against insecurity, against injustice, in which multitudes of persons have found full opportunity for the exercise of their combative tendencies.

The time may be far off when men will cease to fulfill their need for combat by destroying each other and when they will manifest it in common and combined efforts against the forces that are enemies of all men equally. But the difficulties in the way are found in the persistence of certain acquired social customs and not in the unchangeability of the demand for combat.

Pugnacity and fear are native elements of human nature. But so are pity and sympathy. We send nurses and physicians to the battlefield and provide hospital facilities as "naturally" as we change bayonets and discharge machine guns. In early times there was a close connection between pugnacity and fighting, for the latter was done largely with the fists. Pugnacity plays a small part in generating wars today. Citizens of one country do not hate those of another nation by instinct. When they attack or are attacked, they do not use their fists in close combat, but throw shells from a great distance at persons whom they have never seen. In modern wars, anger and hatred come after the war has started; they are effects of war, not the cause of it.

It is a tough job sustaining a modern war; all the emotional reactions have to be excited. Propaganda and atrocity stories are enlisted. Aside from such extreme measures there has to be definite organization, as we saw in the World War, to keep up the morale of even non-combatants. And morale is largely a matter of keeping emotions at a certain pitch; and unfortunately fear, hatred, suspicion, are among the emotions most easily aroused.

I shall not attempt to dogmatize about the causes of modern wars. But I do not think that anyone will deny that they are social rather than psychological, though psychological appeal is highly important in working up a people to the point where they want to fight and in keeping them at it. I do not think, moreover, that anyone will deny that economic conditions are powerful among the social causes of war. The main point, however, is that whatever the sociological causes, they are affairs of tradition, custom, and institutional organization, and these factors belong among the changeable manifestations of human nature, not among the unchangeable elements.

I have used the case of war as a typical instance of what is changeable and what is unchangeable in human nature, in their relation to schemes of social change. I have selected the case because it is an extremely difficult one in which to effect durable changes, not because it is an easy one. The point is that the obstacles in the way are put there by social forces which do change from time to time, not by fixed elements of human nature. This fact is also illustrated in the failures of pacifists to achieve their ends by appeal simply to sympathy and pity. For while, as I have said, the kindly emotions are also a fixed constituent of human nature, the channel they take is dependent upon social conditions.

There is always a great outburst of these kindly emotions in time of war. Fellow feeling and the desire to help those in need are intense during war, as they are at every period of great disaster that comes home to observation or imagination. But they are canalized in their expression; they are confined to those upon our side. They occur simultaneously with manifestation of rage and fear against the other side, if not always in the same person, at least in the community generally. Hence the ultimate failure of pacifist appeals to the kindly elements of native human nature when they are separated from intelligent consideration of the social and economic forces at work.

William James made a great contribution in the title of one of his essays, *The Moral Equivalent of War*. The very title conveys the point I am making. Certain basic needs and emotions are permanent. But they are capable of finding expression in ways that are radically different from the ways in which they now currently operate.

An even more burning issue emerges when there is proposed any fundamental change in economic institutions and relations. Proposals for such sweeping change are among the commonplaces of our time. On the other hand, the proposals are met by the statement that the changes are impossible because they involve an impossible change in human nature. To this statement, advocates of the desired changes are only too likely to reply that the present system or some phase of it is contrary to human nature. The argument *pro* and *con* then gets put on the wrong ground.

As a matter of fact, economic institutions and relations are among the manifestations of human nature that are most susceptible of change. History is living evidence of the scope of these changes. Aristotle, for example, held that paying interest is unnatural, and the Middle Ages reechoed the doctrine. All interest was usury, and it was only after economic conditions had so changed that payment of interest was a customary and in that sense a "natural" thing, that usury got its present meaning.

There have been times and places in which land was held in common and in which private ownership of land would have been regarded as the most monstrous of unnatural things. There have been other times and places when all wealth was possessed by an overlord and his subjects held wealth, if any, subject to his pleasure. The entire system of credit so fundamental in contemporary financial and industrial life is a modern invention. The invention of the joint stock company with limited liability of individuals has brought about a great change from earlier facts and conceptions of property. I think the need of owning something is one of the native elements of human nature. But it takes either ignorance or a very lively fancy to suppose that the system of ownership that exists in the United States in 1938, with all its complex relations and its interweaving with legal and political supports, is a necessary and unchangeable product of an inherent tendency to appropriate and possess.

Law is one of the most conservative of human institutions; yet through the cumulative effect of legislation and judicial decisions it changes, sometimes at a slow rate, sometimes rapidly. The changes in human relations that are brought about by changes in industrial and legal institutions then react to modify the ways in which human nature manifests itself, and this brings about still further changes in institutions, and so on indefinitely.

It is for these reasons that I say that those who hold that proposals for social change, even of rather a profound character, are impossible and utopian because of the fixity of human nature, confuse the resistance to change that comes from acquired habits with that which comes from original human nature. The savage, living in a primitive society, comes nearer to being a purely "natural" human being than does civilized man. Civilization itself is the product of altered human nature. But even the savage is bound by a mass of tribal customs and transmitted beliefs that modify his original nature, and it is these acquired habits that make it so difficult to transform him into a civilized human being.

The revolutionary radical, on the other hand, overlooks the force of engrained habits. He is right, in my opinion, about the indefinite plasticity of human nature. But he is wrong in thinking that patterns of desire, belief, and purpose do not have a force comparable to the momentum of physical objects once they are set in motion, and comparable to the inertia, the resistance to movement, possessed by these same objects when they are at rest. Habit, not original human nature, keeps things moving most of the time, about as they have moved in the past.

If human nature is unchangeable, then there is no such thing as education and all our efforts to educate are doomed to failure. For the very meaning of education is modification of native human nature in formation of those new ways of thinking, of feeling, of desiring, and of believing that are foreign to raw human nature. If the latter were unalterable, we might have training but not education. For training, as distinct from education, means simply the acquisition of certain skills. Native gifts can be trained to a point of higher efficiency without that development of new attitudes and dispositions which is the goal of education. But the result is mechanical. It is like supposing that while a musician may acquire by practice greater technical ability, he cannot rise from one plane of musical appreciation and creation to another.

The theory that human nature is unchangeable is thus the most depressing and pessimistic of all possible doctrines. If it were carried out logically, it would mean a doctrine of predestination from birth that would outdo the most rigid of theological doctrines. For according to it, persons are what they are at birth and nothing can be done about it, beyond the kind of training that an acrobat might give to the muscular system with which he is originally endowed. If a person is born with criminal tendencies, a criminal he will become and remain. If a person is born with an excessive amount of greed, he will become a person living by predatory activities at the expense of others; and so on. I do not doubt at all the existence of differences in natural endowment. But what I am questioning is the notion that they doom individuals to a fixed channel of expression. It is difficult indeed to make a silk purse out of a sow's ear. But the particular form which, say, a natural musical endowment will take depends upon the social influences to which it is subjected. Beethoven in a savage tribe would doubtless have been outstanding as a musician, but he would not have been the Beethoven who composed symphonies.

The existence of almost every conceivable kind of social institution at some time and place in the history of the world is evidence of the plasticity of human nature. This fact does not prove that all these different social systems are of equal value, materially, morally, and culturally. The slightest observation shows that such is not the case. But the fact in proving the changeability of human nature indicates the attitude that should be taken toward proposals for social changes. The question is primarily whether they, in special cases, are desirable or not. And the way to answer that question is to try to discover what their consequences would be if they were adopted. Then if the conclusion is that they are desirable, the further question is how they can be accomplished with a minimum of waste, destruction, and needless dislocation.

In finding the answer to this question, we have to take into account the force of existing traditions and customs; of the patterns of action and belief that already exist. We have to find out what forces already at work can be reinforced so that they move toward the desired change and how the conditions that oppose change can be gradually weakened. Such questions as these can be considered on the basis of fact and reason.

The assertion that a proposed change is impossible because of the fixed constitution of human nature diverts attention from the question of whether or not a change is desirable and from the other question of how it shall be brought about. It throws the question into the arena of blind emotion and brute force. In the end, it encourages those who think that great changes can be produced offhand and by the use of sheer violence.

When our sciences of human nature and human relations are anything like as developed as are our sciences of physical nature, their chief concern will be with the problem of how human nature is most effectively modified. The question will not be whether it is capable of change, but of how it is to be changed under given conditions. This problem is ultimately that of education in its widest sense. Consequently, whatever represses and distorts the processes of education that might bring about a change in human dispositions with the minimum of waste puts a premium upon the forces that bring society to a state of deadlock, and thereby encourages the use of violence as a means of social change.

ARISTOTLE

The Good

Plato's student, Aristotle, was born at Stagira in Thrace in 384 B.C., the son of the family physician to the king of Macedonia. He entered Plato's Academy in Athens at the age of eighteen and remained there until Plato's death nineteen years later. Aristotle then left Athens, studied and traveled for nearly twelve years, three of which were spent tutoring the future Alexander the Great. After returning to Athens in 335 B.C. Aristotle founded the Lyceum and turned his talents to teaching and writing such works as Metaphysics, Nicomachean Ethics, Politics, *and* Poetics. *When Alexander died in 323* B.C., *the Athenians brought a charge of impiety against the philosopher. To escape the fate of Socrates, Aristotle fled to Chalcis, where he died a short time later.*

Aristotle begins, in a way characteristic of his method, with a generalization which, if accepted, will lead to a more exact account of his subject. It is a generalization which is fundamental to his philosophy and in his own mind there is no doubt about the truth of it. Yet he is not at this point asserting its truth. He is content to state a position which he has found reason to hold. It may be defined in some such words as these: The good is that at which all things aim. *If we are to understand this, we must form to ourselves a clear notion of what is meant by an aim or, in more technical language, an 'end'. The first chapter of the* Ethics *is concerned with making the notion clear.* [—Trans.]

It is thought that every activity, artistic or scientific, in fact every deliberate action or pursuit, has for its object the attainment of some good. We may therefore assent to the view which has been expressed that 'the good' is 'that at which all things aim'.[1]

From *The Ethics of Aristotle*, trans. J. A. K. Thomson (Baltimore: Penguin Books, Inc., 1955), pp. 25, 30, 62–66, 73–75, 227–228, 303–305. Used by permission of George Allen & Unwin Ltd., London.

[1] It is of course obvious that to a certain extent they do not all aim at the same thing, for in some cases the end will be an activity, in others the product which goes beyond the actual activity. In the arts which aim at results of this kind the results or products are intrinsically superior to the activities.

Since modes of action involving the practised hand and the instructed brain are numerous, the number of their ends is proportionately large. For instance, the end of medical science is health; of military science, victory; of economic science, wealth. All skills of that kind which come under a single 'faculty'—a skill in making bridles or any other part of a horse's gear comes under the faculty or art of horsemanship, while horsemanship itself and every branch of military practice comes under the art of war, and in like manner other arts and techniques are subordinate to yet others—in all these the ends of the master arts are to be preferred to those of the subordinate skills, for it is the former that provide the motive for pursuing the latter.[2]

Now if there is an end which as moral agents we seek for its own sake, and which is the cause of our seeking all the other ends—if we are not to go on choosing one act for the sake of another, thus landing ourselves in an infinite progression with the result that desire will be frustrated and ineffectual—it is clear that this must be the good, that is the absolutely good. May we not then argue from this that a knowledge of the good is a great advantage to us in the conduct of our lives? Are we not more likely to hit the mark if we have a target? If this be true, we must do our best to get at least a rough idea of what the good really is, and which of the sciences, pure or applied, is concerned with the business of achieving it. . . .

A man's way of life may afford a clue to his genuine views upon the nature of happiness. It is therefore worth our while to glance at the different types of life. [—Trans.]

There is a general assumption that the manner of a man's life is a clue to what he on reflection regards as the good—in other words, happiness. Persons of low tastes (always in the majority) hold that it is pleasure. Accordingly they ask for nothing better than the sort of life which consists in having a good time. (I have in mind the three well-known types of life—that just mentioned, that of the man of affairs, that of the philosophic student.) The utter vulgarity of the herd of men comes out in their preference for the sort of existence a cow leads. Their view would hardly get

---

[2] It makes no difference if the ends of the activities are the activities themselves or something over and above these, as in the case of the sciences I have mentioned.

a respectful hearing, were it not that those who occupy great positions sympathize with a monster of sensuality like Sardanapalus. The gentleman, however, and the man of affairs identify the good with honour, which may fairly be described as the end which men pursue in political or public life. Yet honour is surely too superficial a thing to be the good we are seeking. Honour depends more on those who confer than on him who receives it, and we cannot but feel that the good is something personal and almost inseparable from its possessor. Again, why do men seek honour? Surely in order to confirm the favourable opinion they have formed of themselves. It is at all events by intelligent men who know them personally that they seek to be honoured. And for what? For their moral qualities. The inference is clear; public men prefer virtue to honour. It might therefore seem reasonable to suppose that virtue rather than honour is the end pursued in the life of the public servant. But clearly even virtue cannot be quite the end. It is possible, most people think, to possess virtue while you are asleep, to possess it without acting under its influence during any portion of one's life. Besides, the virtuous man may meet with the most atrocious luck or ill-treatment; and nobody, who was not arguing for argument's sake, would maintain that a man with an existence of that sort was 'happy'. The third type of life is the 'contemplative', and this we shall discuss later.

As for the life of the business man, it does not give him much freedom of action. Besides, wealth obviously is not the good we seek, for the sole purpose it serves is to provide the means of getting something else. So far as that goes, the ends we have already mentioned would have a better title to be considered the good, for they are desired on their own account. But in fact even their claim must be disallowed. We may say that they have furnished the ground for many arguments and leave the matter at that.

It is now time to produce a formal definition of virtue. In the Aristotelian system this means stating its genus and differentia—that is to say, the class of things to which it belongs and the point or points which distinguish it from other members of the class. [—Trans.]

We now come to the formal definition of virtue. Note first, however, that the human soul is conditioned in three ways. It may have

(1) feelings, (2) capacities, (3) dispositions; so virtue must be one of these three. By 'feelings' I mean desire, anger, fear, daring, envy, gratification, friendliness, hatred, longing, jealousy, pity and in general all states of mind that are attended by pleasure or pain. By 'capacities' I mean those faculties in virtue of which we may be described as capable of the feelings in question—anger, for instance, or pain, or pity. By 'dispositions' I mean states of mind in virtue of which we are well or ill disposed in respect of the feelings concerned. We have, for instance, a bad disposition where angry feelings are concerned if we are disposed to become excessively or insufficiently angry, and a good disposition in this respect if we consistently feel the due amount of anger, which comes between these extremes. So with the other feelings.

Now, neither the virtues nor the vices are feelings. We are not spoken of as good or bad in respect of our feelings but of our virtues and vices. Neither are we praised or blamed for the way we feel. A man is not praised for being frightened or angry, nor is he blamed just for being angry; it is for being angry in a particular way. But we *are* praised and blamed for our virtues and vices. Again, feeling angry or frightened is something we can't help, but our virtues are in a manner expressions of our will; at any rate there is an element of will in their formation. Finally, we are said to be 'moved' when our feelings are affected, but when it is a question of moral goodness or badness we are not said to be 'moved' but to be 'disposed' in a particular way. A similar line of reasoning will prove that the virtues and vices are not capacities either. We are not spoken of as good or bad, nor are we praised or blamed, merely because we are *capable* of feeling. Again, what capacities we have, we have by nature; but it is not nature that makes us good or bad. . . . So, if the virtues are neither feelings nor capacities, it remains that they must be dispositions. . . .

We have now to state the 'differentia' of virtue. Virtue is a disposition; but how are we to distinguish it from other dispositions? We may say that it is such a disposition as enables the good man to perform his function well. And he performs it well when he avoids the extremes and chooses the mean in actions and feelings. [—Trans.]

It is not, however, enough to give this account of the *genus* of virtue—that it is a disposition; we must describe its *species*. Let us begin, then, with this proposition. Excellence of whatever kind affects that of which it is the excellence in two ways. (1) It produces a good state in it. (2) It enables it to perform its function well. Take eyesight. The goodness of your eye is not only that which makes your eye good, it is also that which makes it function well. Or take the case of a horse. The goodness of a horse makes him a good horse, but it also makes him good at running, carrying a rider, and facing the enemy. Our proposition, then, seems to be true, and it enables us to say that virtue in a man will be the disposition which (a) makes him a good man, (b) enables him to perform his function well. We have already touched on this point, but more light will be thrown upon it if we consider what is the specific nature of virtue.

Virtue

Every form, then, of applied knowledge, when it performs its function well, looks to the mean and works to the standard set by that. It is because people feel this that they apply the *cliché*, 'You couldn't add anything to it or take anything from it' to an artistic masterpiece, the implication being that too much and too little alike destroy perfection, while the mean preserves it. Now if this be so, and if it be true, as we say, that good craftsmen work to the standard of the mean, then, since goodness like Nature is more exact and of a higher character than any art, it follows that goodness is the quality that hits the mean. By 'goodness' I mean goodness of moral character, since it is moral goodness that deals with feelings and actions, and it is in them that we find excess, deficiency, and a mean. It is possible, for example, to experience fear, boldness, desire, anger, pity, and pleasures and pains generally, too much or too little or to the right amount. If we feel them too much or too little, we are wrong. But to have these feelings at the right times on the right occasions towards the right people for the right motive and in the right way is to have them in the right measure, that is, somewhere between the extremes; and this is what characterizes goodness. The same may be said of the mean and extremes in actions. Now it is in the field of actions and feelings that goodness operates; in them we find excess, deficiency, and, between them, the mean, the first two being wrong, the mean right and praised as such.³ Goodness, then, is a mean condition in the sense that it aims at and hits the mean. . . .

I have said enough to show that moral excellence is a mean, and I have shown in what sense it is so. It is, namely, a mean between two forms of badness, one of excess and the other of defect, and is so described because it aims at hitting the mean point in feelings and in actions. This makes virtue hard of achievement, because finding the middle point is never easy. It is not everybody, for instance, who can find the centre of a circle—that calls for a geometrician. Thus, too, it is easy to fly into a passion—anybody can do that—but to be angry with the right person and to the right extent and at the right time and with the right object and in the right way—that is not easy, and it is not everyone who can do it. This is equally true of giving or spending money. Hence we infer that to do these things properly is rare, laudable and fine.

Aristotle now suggests some rules for our guidance. [—Trans.]

In view of this we shall find it useful when aiming at the mean to observe these rules. (1) *Keep away from that extreme which is the more opposed to the mean.* It is Calypso's advice:

Swing round the ship clear of this surf and surge.

For one of the extremes is always a more dangerous error than the other; and—since it is hard to hit the bull's-eye—we must take the next best course and choose the least of the evils. And it will be easiest for us to do this if we follow the rule I have suggested. (2) *Note the errors into which we personally are most liable to fall.* (Each of us has his natural bias in one direction or another.) We shall find out what ours are by noting what gives us pleasure and pain. After that we must drag ourselves in the opposite direction. For our best way of reaching the middle is by giving a wide berth to our darling sin. It is the method used by a carpenter when he is straightening a warped board. (3) *Always be particularly on your guard against pleasure and pleasant things.* When Pleasure is at the bar the jury is not impartial. So it will be best for us if we feel towards her as the Trojan elders felt towards Helen, and regularly apply their words to her. If we are for packing her off, as they were with Helen, we shall be the less likely to go wrong.

³ Being right or successful and being praised are both indicative of excellence.

To sum up. These are the rules by observation of which we have the best chance of hitting the mean. But of course difficulties spring up, especially when we are confronted with an exceptional case. For example, it is not easy to say precisely what is the right way to be angry and with whom and on what grounds and for how long. In fact we are inconsistent on this point, sometimes praising people who are deficient in the capacity for anger and calling them 'gentle', sometimes praising the choleric and calling them 'stout fellows'. To be sure we are not hard on a man who goes off the straight path in the direction of too much or too little, if he goes off only a little way. We reserve our censure for the man who swerves widely from the course, because then we are bound to notice it. Yet it is not easy to find a formula by which we may determine how far and up to what point a man may go wrong before he incurs blame. But this difficulty of definition is inherent in every object of perception; such questions of degree are bound up with the circumstances of the individual case, where our only criterion *is* the perception.

So much, then, has become clear. In all our conduct it is the mean state that is to be praised. But one should lean sometimes in the direction of the more, sometimes in that of the less, because that is the readiest way of attaining to goodness and the mean. . . .

Friendship and Happiness

Our next subject must be friendship. This is necessary because such love has somewhat the character of a virtue, or at any rate involves virtue. Besides, it is one of the things which life can least afford to be without. No one would choose a friendless existence on condition of having all the other good things in the world. So true is this, that the rich and men in positions of authority and power are believed to stand, more than other people, in need of friends. For what would they get out of their prosperity if they were deprived of the chance of performing those offices of kindness for which their friends supply them with the greatest and most laudable opportunities? Or how could their prosperity be guarded and preserved, if they had no friends? For the greater prosperity is, the more precarious. In poverty also and all the other misfortunes of life the thoughts of men turn to their friends as their one refuge. Truly friends are an aid—to the young in keeping them from making mistakes; to the old in supplying their wants and doing for them what in the failure of their physical powers they cannot do for themselves; to those in the prime of life by making it possible for them to get fine achievements brought to accomplishment. Two are better than one, or (as Homer puts it)

When two upon a journey go, one sees before the other.

For indeed two are better able to 'see' a thing and to do it than is one.

Then the feeling, which we find not only among men but among birds and most animals, of parent towards offspring, and offspring towards parent, seems to have been implanted by nature. We must say the same of the feeling between creatures of the same species, more particularly the human species. Friendship then, being a necessity of human nature, is a good thing and a precious. So we praise those who love their fellow-men. And one notices in one's travels how everybody feels that everybody else is his friend and brother man. Again, it is pretty clear that those who frame the constitutions of states set more store by this feeling than by justice itself. For their two prime objectives are to expel faction, which is inspired by hate, and to produce concord—concord being like friendship. Between friends there is no need of justice, though men can be just and yet lacking in friendly feeling, which some go so far as to think an element in the highest form of justice, which we saw to be equity. It is not only that friendship is necessary to the good life, it is in itself a good and beautiful thing. We praise a man for loving his friends, and the possession of many has always been considered one of the things that ennoble existence. Nay, some even believe that to be a friend you must also be a good man. . . .

Aristotle gives reasons for thinking that Happiness in its highest and best manifestation is found in cultivating the 'contemplative' life. [—Trans.]

But if happiness is an activity in accordance with virtue, it is reasonable to assume that it will be in accordance with the highest virtue; and this can only be the virtue of the best part of us. Whether this be the intellect or something else—whatever it is that is held to have a natural right to govern and guide us, and to have an insight into what is noble and divine, either as being itself also divine or more divine than any other part of us—it is the activity of this part in accordance with the virtue proper to it that will be perfect happiness. Now we have seen already that this activity has a speculative or contemplative character. This is a conclusion which may be accepted as in harmony with our earlier arguments and with the truth. For 'contemplation' is the highest form of activity, since the intellect is the highest thing in us and the objects which come within its range are the highest that can be known. But it is also the most continuous activity, for we can think about intellectual problems more continuously than we can keep up any sort of physical action. Again, we feel sure that a modicum of pleasure must be one of the ingredients of happiness. Now it is admitted that activity along the lines of 'wisdom' is the pleasantest of all the good activities. At all events it is thought that philosophy ('the pursuit of wisdom') has pleasures marvellous in purity and duration, and it stands to reason that those who have knowledge pass their time more pleasantly than those who are engaged in its pursuit. Again, self-sufficiency will be found to belong in an exceptional degree to the exercise of the speculative intellect. The wise man, as much as the just man and everyone else, must have the necessaries of life. But, given an adequate supply of these, the just man also needs people with and towards whom he can put his justice into operation; and we can use similar language about the temperate man, the brave man, and so on. But the wise man can do more. He can speculate all by himself, and the wiser he is the better he can do it. Doubtless it helps to have fellow-workers, but for all that he is the most self-sufficing of men. Finally it may well be thought that the activity of contemplation is the only one that is praised on its own account, because nothing comes of it beyond the act of contemplation, whereas from practical activities we count on gaining something more or less over and above the mere action. Again, it is commonly believed that, to have happiness, one must have leisure; we occupy ourselves in order that we may have leisure, just as we make war for the sake of peace. Now the practical virtues find opportunity for their exercise in politics and in war, but these are occupations which are supposed to leave no room for leisure. Certainly it is true of the trade of war, for no one deliberately chooses to make war for the sake of making it or tries to bring about a war. A man would be regarded as a blood-thirsty monster if he were to make war on a friendly state just to produce battles and slaughter. The business of the politician also makes leisure impossible. Besides the activity itself, politics aims at securing positions of power and honour or the happiness of the politician himself or his fellow-citizens—a happiness obviously distinct from that which we are seeking.

IMMANUEL KANT

The Incentive to Morality

Immanuel Kant was born in Königsberg, Prussia, in 1724, of a poor and deeply religious Pietist family and remained in the Königsberg area until his death eighty years later. He was educated at a Pietist school for seven years before entering the University of Königsberg, where he studied philosophy and mathematics and partially supported himself by tutoring other students. When his father died in 1746, Kant left the university for nine years, during which time he served as a resident tutor for several families. In 1755 the most important of his early scientific writings was published, General Natural History and Theory of the Heavens, *and he returned to the university as a lecturer on a number of subjects. He became Professor of Logic and Metaphysics in 1770 and held this position until his retirement. Kant never married, followed a daily regimen so strict that people were said to set their watches by his routine, and became the best-known professor in Germany with works such as* Critique of Pure Reason *(1781),* Foundations of the Metaphysic of Morals *(1785),* Critique of Practical Reason *(1788),* Critique of Judgment *(1790), and* Perpetual Peace *(1795).*

In the subject there is no antecedent feeling tending to morality; that is impossible, because all feeling is sensuous, and the incentives of the moral disposition must be free from every sensuous condition. Rather, sensuous feeling, which is the basis of all our inclinations, is the condition of the particular feeling we call respect, but the cause that determines this feeling lies in the pure practical reason; because of its origin, therefore, this particular feeling cannot be said to be pathologically effected; rather, it is practically effected. Since the idea of the moral law deprives self-love of its influence and self-conceit of its delusion, it lessens the obstacle to pure practical reason and produces the idea of the superiority of its objective law to the impulses of sensibility; it increases the weight of the moral law by removing, in the judgment of reason, the counterweight to the moral law which bears on a will affected by the sensibility. Thus respect for the law is not the incentive to morality;

From Immanuel Kant, *Critique of Practical Reason*, trans. Lewis White Beck, pp. 78–81, 85–87, 90–91, 30–31, 36–41, copyright © 1956 by The Liberal Arts Press; reprinted by permission of The Liberal Arts Press Div. of The Bobbs-Merrill Co., Inc.

it is morality itself, regarded subjectively as an incentive, inasmuch as pure practical reason, by rejecting all the rival claims of self-love, gives authority and absolute sovereignty to the law. It should be noticed that, as respect is an effect on feeling and thus on the sensibility of a rational being, it presupposes the sensuousness and hence the finitude of such beings on whom respect for the moral law is imposed; thus respect for the law cannot be attributed to a supreme being or even to one free from all sensibility, since to such a being there could be no obstacle to practical reason.

This feeling, under the name of moral feeling, is therefore produced solely by reason. It does not serve for an estimation of actions or as a basis of the objective moral law itself but only as an incentive to make this law itself a maxim. By what name better than moral feeling could we call this singular feeling, which cannot be compared with any pathological feeling? It is of such a peculiar kind that it seems to be at the disposal only of reason, and indeed only of the pure practical reason.

Respect always applies to persons only, never to things. The latter can awaken inclinations, and even love if they are animals (horses, dogs, etc.), or fear, as does the sea, a volcano, or a beast of prey; but they never arouse respect. Something which approaches this feeling is admiration, and this, as an emotion (astonishment) can refer also to things, e.g., lofty mountains, the magnitude, number, and distance of the heavenly bodies, the strength and swiftness of many animals, etc. All of this, however, is not respect. A man can also be an object of love, fear, or admiration even to astonishment, and yet not be an object of respect. His jocular humor, his courage and strength, and his power of rank may inspire me with such feelings, though inner respect for him is still lacking. Fontenelle says, "I bow to a great man, but my mind does not bow." I can add: to a humble plain man, in whom I perceive righteousness in a higher degree than I am conscious of in myself, *my mind bows* whether I choose or not, however high I carry my head that he may not forget my superior position. Why? His example holds a law before me which strikes down my self-conceit when I compare my own conduct with it; that it is a law which can be obeyed, and consequently is one that can actually be put into practice, is proved to my eyes by the act. I may even be conscious of a like degree of righteousness in myself, and yet respect remains. In men all good is defective, but the law made visible in an example always humbles my pride, since the man whom I see before me provides me with a standard by clearly appearing to me in a more favorable light in spite of his imperfections, which, though perhaps always with him, are not so well known to me as are my own. Respect is a tribute we cannot refuse to pay to merit whether we will or not; we can indeed outwardly withhold it, but we cannot help feeling it inwardly.

Respect is so far from being a feeling of pleasure that one only reluctantly gives way to it as regards a man. We seek to discover something that will lighten the burden of it for us, some fault to compensate us for the humiliation which we suffer from such an example. The dead themselves are not immune from this criticism, especially when their example appears inimitable. Even the moral law itself in its solemn majesty is exposed to this endeavor to keep one's self from yielding respect to it. Can it be thought that there is any reason why we like to degrade it to the level of our familiar inclination and why we take so much trouble to make it the chosen precept of our well-understood interest, other than the fact that we want to be free of the awesome respect which so severely shows us our own unworthiness? Nevertheless, there is on the other hand so little displeasure in it that, when once we renounce our self-conceit and respect has established its practical influence, we cannot ever satisfy ourselves in contemplating the majesty of this law, and the soul believes itself to be elevated in proportion as it sees the holy law as elevated over it and its frail nature. Certainly, great talents and activity proportionate to them can occasion respect or an analogous feeling, and it is proper to accord it to them; then it seems that admiration is the same as this feeling [of respect]. But if one looks more closely it is noticed that it is always uncertain how great a part of the ability must be ascribed to innate talent and how much to cultivation through the person's own diligence. Presumably reason represents it to us as a fruit of cultivation, and therefore as merit which perceptibly diminishes our self-conceit and therefore either reproaches us or imposes it upon us as an example to be followed. This respect which we have for a person (really for the law, which his example holds before us) is, therefore, not mere admiration. This is also confirmed by the way the common run of men give up their respect for a man (e.g., Voltaire) when they think they have in some manner found the badness of his character, while the true scholar still feels this respect at least for his talents, since he is himself involved in a business and vocation which makes imitation of him to some extent a law.

Respect for the moral law is therefore the sole and undoubted moral incentive, and this feeling is directed to no being except on this basis. . . .

It is a very beautiful thing to do good to men because of love and a sympathetic good will, or to do justice because of a love of order. But this is not the genuine moral maxim of our conduct, the maxim which is suitable to our position among rational beings as men, when we presume, like volunteers, to flout with proud conceit the thought of duty and, as independent of command, merely to will of our own good pleasure to do something to which we think we need no command. We stand under a *discipline* of reason, and in all our maxims we must not forget our subjection to it, or withdraw anything from it, or by an egotistical illusion detract from the authority of the law (even though it is given by our own reason), so that we could place the determining ground of our will (even though it is in accordance with the law) elsewhere than in the law itself and in respect for it. Duty and obligation are the only names which we must give to our relation to the moral law. We are indeed legislative members of a moral realm which is possible through freedom and which is presented to us as an object of respect by practical reason; yet we are at the same time subjects in it, not sovereigns, and to mistake our inferior position as creatures and to deny, from self-conceit, respect to the holy law is, in spirit, a defection from it even if its letter be fulfilled.

The possibility of such a command as, "Love God above all and thy neighbor as thyself,"[1] agrees very well with this. For, as a command, it requires respect for a law which orders love and does not leave it to arbitrary choice to make love the principle. But love to God as inclination (pathological love) is impossible, for He is not an object of the senses. The latter is indeed possible toward men, but it cannot be commanded, for it is not possible for man to love someone merely on command. It is, therefore, only practical love which can be understood in that kernel of all laws. To love God means in this sense to like to do His commandments, and to

[1] The principle of one's own happiness, which some wish to make the supreme principle of morality, is in striking contrast to this law. This principle would read: "Love thyself above all, but God and thy neighbor for thine own sake."

love one's neighbor means to like to practice all duties toward him. The command which makes this a rule cannot require that we have this disposition but only that we endeavor after it. To command that one do something gladly is self-contradictory. For a law would not be needed if we already knew of ourselves what we ought to do and moreover were conscious of liking to do it; and if we did it without liking but only out of respect for the law, a command which makes just this respect the incentive of the maxim would counteract the disposition it commands. That law of all laws, like every moral prescription of the Gospel, thus presents the moral disposition in its complete perfection, and though as an ideal of holiness it is unattainable by any creature, it is yet an archetype which we should strive to approach and to imitate in an uninterrupted infinite progress. If a rational creature could ever reach the stage of thoroughly liking to do all moral laws, it would mean that there was no possibility of there being in him a desire which could tempt him to deviate from them, for overcoming such a desire always costs the subject some sacrifice and requires self-compulsion, i.e., an inner constraint to do that which one does not quite like to do. To such a level of moral disposition no creature can ever attain. For since he is a creature, and consequently is always dependent with respect to what he needs for complete satisfaction with his condition, he can never be wholly free from desires and inclinations which, because they rest on physical causes, do not of themselves agree with the moral law, which has an entirely different source. Consequently, it is with reference to these desires always necessary to base the intention of the creature's maxims on moral constraint and not on ready willingness, i.e., to base it on respect which demands obedience to the law even though the creature does not like to do it, and not on love, which apprehends no inward reluctance to the law by the will. . . .

The moral law is holy (inviolable). Man is certainly unholy enough, but humanity in his person must be holy to him. Everything in creation which he wishes and over which he has power can be used merely as a means; only man, and, with him, every rational creature, is an end in itself. He is the subject of the moral law which is holy, because of the autonomy of his freedom. Because of the latter, every will, even the private will of each person directed to himself, is restricted to the condition of agreement with the autonomy of the rational being, namely, that it be subjected to no purpose which is not possible by a law which could arise from the will of the passive subject itself. This condition thus requires that the person never be used as a means except when he is at the same an end. We may rightly attribute this condition even to the divine will with respect to the rational beings in the world as its creatures, since the condition rests on the personality of these beings, whereby alone they are ends in themselves.

This idea of personality awakens respect; it places before our eyes the sublimity of our own nature (in its [higher] vocation), while it shows us at the same time the unsuitability of our conduct to it, thus striking down our self-conceit. This is naturally and easily observed by the most common human reason. Has not every even fairly honest man sometimes found that he desists from an otherwise harmless lie which would extricate him from a vexing affair or which would even be useful to a beloved and deserving friend simply in order not to have to contemn himself secretly in his own eyes? In the greatest misfortunes of his life which he could have avoided if he could have disregarded duty, does not a righteous man hold up his head thanks to the consciousness that he has honored and preserved humanity in his own person and in its dignity, so that he does not have to shame himself in his own eyes or have reason to fear the inner scrutiny of self-examination? This comfort is not happiness, not even the smallest part of happiness; for no one would wish to have occasion for it, not even once in his life, or perhaps would even desire life itself in such circumstances. But he lives and cannot tolerate seeing himself as unworthy of life. This inner satisfaction is therefore merely negative with reference to everything which might make life pleasant; it is the defense against the danger of sinking in personal worth after the value of his circumstances has been completely lost. It is the effect of a respect for something entirely different from life, in comparison and contrast to which life and its enjoyment have absolutely no worth. He yet lives only because it is his duty, not because he has the least taste for living. . . .

FUNDAMENTAL LAW OF PURE PRACTICAL REASON

So act that the maxim of your will could always hold at the same time as a principle establishing universal law.

Pure geometry has postulates as practical propositions, which, however, contain nothing more than the presupposition that one *can* do something and that, when some result is needed, one *should* do it; these are the only propositions of pure geometry which apply to an existing thing. They are thus practical rules under a problematic condition of the will. Here, however, the rule says: One ought absolutely to act in a certain way. The practical rule is therefore unconditional and thus is thought of a priori as a categorically practical proposition. . . .

When one's own happiness is made the determining ground of the will, the result is the direct opposite of the principle of morality; and I have previously shown that, whenever the determining ground which is to serve as a law is located elsewhere than in the legislative form of the maxim, we have to reckon with this result. . . .
Suppose that an acquaintance whom you otherwise liked were to attempt to justify himself before you for having borne false witness by appealing to what he regarded as the holy duty of consulting his own happiness and, then, by recounting all the advantages he had gained thereby, pointing out the prudence he had shown in securing himself against detection, even by yourself, to whom alone he now reveals the secret only in order that he may be able at any time to deny it. And suppose that he then affirmed, in all seriousness, that he had thereby fulfilled a true human duty—you would either laugh in his face or shrink from him in disgust, even though you would not have the least grounds for objecting to such measures if a man regulated his principles solely with a view to his own advantage. Or suppose someone recommends to you as steward a man to whom you could blindly trust your affairs and, in order to inspire you with confidence, further extols him as a prudent man who has a masterly understanding of his own interest and is so indefatigably active that he misses no opportunity to further it; furthermore, lest you should be afraid of finding a vulgar selfishness in him, he praises the good taste with which he lives, not seeking his pleasure in making money or in coarse wantonness, but in the increase of his knowledge, in instructive conversation with a select circle, and even in relieving the needy. But, he adds, he is not particular as to the means (which, of course, derive their value only from the end), being as willing to use another's money and property as his own, provided only that he knows he can do so safely and without discovery. You would believe that the person making such a recommendation was either mocking you or had lost his mind. So

distinct and sharp are the boundaries between morality and self-love that even the commonest eye cannot fail to distinguish whether a thing belongs to one or the other. The few remarks which follow may appear superfluous where the truth is so obvious, but they serve at least to furnish somewhat greater distinctness to the judgment of common sense.

The principle of happiness can indeed give maxims, but never maxims which are competent to be laws of the will, even if universal happiness were made the object. For, since the knowledge of this rests on mere data of experience, as each judgment concerning it depends very much on the very changeable opinion of each person, it can give general but never universal rules; that is, the rules it gives will on the average be most often the right ones for this purpose, but they will not be rules which must hold always and necessarily. Consequently, no practical laws can be based on this principle. . . .

The maxim of self-love (prudence) merely advises; the law of morality commands. Now there is a great difference between that which we are advised to do and that which we are obligated to do.

What is required in accordance with the principle of autonomy of choice is easily and without hesitation seen by the commonest intelligence; what is to be done under the presupposition of its heteronomy is hard to see and requires knowledge of the world. That is to say, what duty is, is plain of itself to everyone, but what is to bring true, lasting advantage to our whole existence is veiled in impenetrable obscurity, and much prudence is required to adapt the practical rule based upon it even tolerably to the ends of life by making suitable exceptions to it. But the moral law commands the most unhesitating obedience from everyone; consequently, the decision as to what is to be done in accordance with it must not be so difficult that even the commonest and most unpracticed understanding without any worldly prudence should go wrong in making it.

It is always in everyone's power to satisfy the commands of the categorical command of morality [viz., the fundamental law of pure practical reason; this is but seldom possible with respect to the empirically conditioned precept of happiness, and it is far from being possible, even in respect to a single purpose, for everyone. The reason is that in the former it is only a question of the maxim, which must be genuine and pure, but in the latter it is also a question of capacity and physical ability to realize a desired object. A command that everyone should seek to make himself happy would be foolish, for no one commands another to do what he already invariably wishes to do. . . .

He who has lost at play may be vexed at himself and his imprudence; but when he is conscious of having cheated at play, even though he has won, he must despise himself as soon as he compares himself with the moral law. This must therefore be something else than the principle of one's own happiness. For to have to say to himself, "I am a worthless man, though I've filled my purse," he must have a different criterion of judgment than if he approves of himself and says, "I am a prudent man, for I've enriched my treasure.". . .

More refined [than the doctrine which makes morality depend on happiness] but equally untrue, is the pretense of those who assume a certain particular moral sense which, instead of reason, determines the moral law, and in accordance with which the consciousness of virtue is directly associated with satisfaction and enjoyment, while consciousness of vice is associated with mental restlessness and pain. Thus everything is reduced to the desire for one's own happiness. Without repeating what has already been said, I will only indicate the fallacy they fall into. In order to imagine the vicious person as tormented with mortification by the consciousness of his transgressions, they must presuppose that he is, in the core of his character, at least to a certain degree morally good, just as they have to think of the person who is delighted by the consciousness of doing dutiful acts as already virtuous. Therefore, the concept of morality and duty must precede all reference to this satisfaction and cannot be derived from it. One must already value the importance of what we call duty, the respect for the moral law, and the immediate worth which a person obtains in his own eyes through obedience to it, in order to feel satisfaction in the consciousness of his conformity to law or the bitter remorse which accompanies his awareness that he has transgressed it. Therefore, this satisfaction of spiritual unrest cannot be felt prior to the knowledge of obligation, nor can it be made the basis of the latter. One must be at least halfway honest even to be able to have an idea of these feelings. For the rest, as the human will, by virtue of its freedom, is directly determined by the moral law, I am far from denying that frequent practice in accordance with this determining ground can itself finally cause a subjective feeling of satisfaction. Indeed, it is a duty to establish and cultivate this feeling, which alone deserves to be called the moral feeling. But the concept of duty cannot be derived from it, for we would have to presuppose a feeling for law as such and regard as an object of sensation what can only be thought by reason. If this did not end up in the flattest contradiction, it would destroy every concept of duty and fill its place with a merely mechanical play of refined inclinations, sometimes contending with the coarser.

JOHN RAWLS

The Sense of Justice

John Rawls was born in Baltimore, Maryland, in 1921, and received his A.B. from Princeton in 1943, his Ph.D. in 1950. In 1952–53, he was a Fulbright Scholar at Oxford and subsequently held a teaching position at Cornell. At present he is Professor of Philosophy at Harvard.

I

In *Émile* Rousseau asserts that the sense of justice is no mere moral conception formed by the understanding alone, but a true sentiment of the heart enlightened by reason, the natural outcome of our primitive affections.[1] In the first part of this paper I set out a psychological construction to illustrate the way in which Rousseau's thesis might be true. In the second part I use several of the ideas elaborated in formulating this construction to consider two questions which arise in the systematic analysis of the concept of justice.

These two questions are: first, to whom is the obligation of justice owed?—that is, in regard to whom must one regulate one's conduct as the principles of justice require?—and second, what accounts for men's doing what justice requires? Very briefly, the answers to these questions are as follows: to the first, the duty of justice is owed to those who are capable of a sense of justice; and to the second, if men did not do what justice requires, not only would they not regard themselves as bound by the principles of justice, but they would be incapable of feeling resentment and indignation, and they would be without ties of friendship and mutual trust. They would lack certain essential elements of humanity.

Throughout, I think of a sense of justice as something which persons have. One refers to it when one says, for example, that cruel and unusual punishments offend one's sense of justice. It may be aroused or assuaged, and it is connected not only with such moral feelings as resentment and indignation but also, as I shall

From John Rawls, "The Sense of Justice," *The Philosophical Review*, **LXXII**, No. 3 (July 1963), pp. 282–293. Used by permission of the editors of *The Philosophical Review* and the author.

[1] Bk. iv, the first part. In the Everyman Edition (London, 1911), see pp. 172–215, in particular pp. 196, 215.

argue, with such natural attitudes as mutual trust and affection. The psychological construction is designed to show how the sense of justice may be viewed as the result of a certain natural development; it will be useful in understanding why the capacity for a sense of justice is the fundamental aspect of moral personality in the theory of justice.

III [2]

The psychological construction by which the sense of justice might develop consists of three parts representing the development of three forms of guilt feelings in this order: authority guilt, association guilt, and principle guilt.[3] There are other forms of guilt feelings, and in other connections it would be essential to discuss them; but for the moment, these other forms may be left aside. The central place given to the feeling of guilt is a matter of convenience and simply a way of arranging what is said about the moral feelings.[4]

To characterize authority guilt, let us suppose an institutional situation in which certain persons are subject to the general precepts or to the particular injunctions of others. The specific case to be taken is the relation of parents and their children. Assume that those subject—the children—love, trust, and have faith in those in authority, the parents. Let us suppose also that those subject are not in a position to question the general precepts or particular injunctions which they are expected to obey, either because they do not have sufficient knowledge and understanding or because they lack the concept of justification, both being the case with children. Suppose, further, to avoid needless complications, that the precepts and injunctions given are reasonable, so that the attitudes of love, trust, and faith are not misplaced. Given these conditions, which involve the natural attitudes of love, trust, and faith within a certain

---

[2] Section II has been omitted.—Ed.

[3] This construction draws upon Jean Piaget's work, *The Moral Judgment of the Child* (London, 1932). It follows the main lines of his account of the development of the sense of justice and incorporates his distinction between the morality of authority and the morality of mutual respect.

[4] In Section VI I shall discuss briefly some of the defining features of the moral feelings, but I do not propose a formal definition of these feelings. For the purpose of the argument it is sufficient to consider them as given by enumeration; and thus as being, for example, the feelings of guilt and remorse, resentment and indignation, and certain forms of shame and contempt.

institutional background, it follows that those subject will manifest what I shall call authority guilt when they violate the precepts set to them.[5] Their action will be recognized and experienced as a breach of the relation of love and trust with the authoritative person. An absence of guilt feelings would betray an absence of love and trust. Guilt feelings are shown (among other ways) in the inclination to confess and to ask forgiveness in order to restore the previous relation; they are part of what defines a relation as one of love and trust.

These remarks require further elaboration. Assume that this psychological law holds: the child, moved by certain instincts and regulated only (if at all) by rational self-love, comes to love, and to recognize the love of, the parent if the parent manifestly loves the child.[6] The parents' love of the child involves an evident intention to care for the child, to do for him as his rational self-love inclines; it involves taking joy in his presence, the support of his sense of competence, and manifest pleasure at his success. One may suppose that in time the love of the parent will foster in the child an equal love for the parent, and that while the capacity for love is innate it requires special circumstances for its development. The parents' love for the child, then, may explain a child's love for his parents; his love for them does not have—indeed, cannot have—a rational explanation in terms of his antecedent instincts and desires. He does not love them in order to insure, say, his security, although he could seem to love them for this reason. That his love of them does not have a rational explanation follows from the concept of love: to love another is to care for him for his own sake as his rational self-love would incline. The child's love of his parents has an explanation—namely, that they first loved him—but not a rational explanation by reference to his original self-love.

If, then, one accepts this psychological principle and assumes that the child's love is an ordered structure of dispositions, or a

[5] The natural attitudes may also be taken as given by enumeration, and thus as being, for example, love and affection, faith and mutual trust. When it is claimed, then, that affection, say, implies a liability to feelings of guilt, this claim depends on the concepts of affection and of guilt feelings. It does not require a definition of a natural attitude and of a moral feeling.

[6] The formulation of this psychological law is drawn from Rousseau's Émile. Rousseau says that while we love from the start what contributes to our preservation, this attachment is quite unconscious and instinctive. What transforms this instinctive liking for others into love is their "evident intention of helping us."

sentiment, how will it show itself? Here it is necessary to keep in mind the peculiar feature of the authority situation: namely, that the child does not have his own standards of criticism. He is not in a position rationally to reject parental injunctions, so that, if he loves and trusts them, he will accept their precepts. He will also strive to live up to them as worthy objects of esteem, and he will accept their way of judging him. He will impose on himself the standards they embody, and he will judge himself as they would when he violates their precepts. The child will do these things, given his peculiar position in the authority situation, if he does, as we assume, love and trust his parents. At the same time, the child is tempted to transgress the parental precepts. He may wish to rebel against their authority which, in so far as the parents succeed in giving him self-esteem, is a humiliating reminder of his dependence. His own desires may exceed the limits of what is permitted, so that the precepts are experienced as unbearable constraints. The child will have feelings of hatred for the parents, but if he loves them, then once he has given in to temptation and violated their injunctions, he will in part take up their attitude toward himself. He will be disposed to reveal his fault by confession and to seek reconciliation. One who is ashamed redeems himself by successful achievement, but one subject to authority guilt wants to be forgiven and to have the previous relation restored. In these various inclinations and their expression are shown the feelings of guilt. Their absence would manifest an absence of love and trust.

IV

The second part of the psychological construction describes the generation of association guilt. The setting of this form of guilt involves the participation in a joint activity of those who regard themselves as associates. These joint activities may take various forms from social institutions proper to games. I assume it is known to all the participants that the rules defining the scheme of co-operation do in fact satisfy the two principles of justice, and I also suppose that the derivation of these principles, as given in the analytic construction, is understood.[7] This knowledge may be more or less intuitive, but I assume that these facts are nevertheless known.

[7] In Section II (omitted), the author proposed to call an institution "just or fair" when it "satisfies the principles which those who participate in it could propose to one another from an original position of equal liberty." The "two

Now let us suppose that, given a system of joint activity meeting these conditions—perhaps some scheme of economic co-operation—the participants are bound by ties of friendship and mutual trust, and rely on one another to do their part. I suppose that these feelings have been generated in any given person by his participating in the activity itself. I assume as a second psychological law that if a person's capacity for fellow-feeling has been realized in accordance with the first law, then, where another, engaged with him in a joint activity known to satisfy the two principles, with evident intention lives up to his duty of fair play, friendly feelings toward him develop as well as feelings of trust and mutual confidence. (One may suppose the participants introduced into the scheme one by one over a period of time, and in this way acquiring these feelings as the others fulfill their duty of fair play.) So if participants in a joint enterprise regularly act with evident intention in accordance with their duty of fair play, they will tend to acquire ties of friendship and mutual trust.

Now given these feelings and relations against the background of a scheme of co-operation known to satisfy the stated conditions, if a person fails to do his part he will experience feelings of association guilt. These feelings will show themselves in various ways: in the inclination to make good the loss to others (reparation) and to admit what one has done and to apologize; in the inclination to ask for reinstatement and to acknowledge and to accept reproofs and penalties; and in a diminished ability to be angry with others should they likewise fail to do their part. The absence of such inclinations would betray the absence of ties of friendship and relations of mutual trust. It would manifest a capacity to associate with others in disregard of those principles which one knows would be mutually acknowledged. It would show that one had no qualms about the losses inflicted on others (or gains taken from them) as

---

principles of justice" for a political or social system are given as follows: "(i) each person participating in it or affected by it has an equal right to the most extensive liberty compatible with a like liberty for all; and (ii) inequalities (as defined and permitted by the pattern of distribution of rights and duties) are arbitrary unless it is reasonable to expect that they will work out for everyone's advantage, and provided that the positions and offices to which they attach, or from which they may be gained, are open to all." For further explanation, see the author's paper, "Justice as Fairness," *Philosophical Review*, LXVII (1958), 164-194.—Ed.

a consequence of one's own acts, and that one was not troubled by the breaches of mutual confidence by which others are deceived. If there are ties of friendship and mutual trust, there exist these various inhibitions and reactions to failing to do one's part. If these inhibitions and reactions are lacking, one has at best only a show of fellow-feeling and mutual trust.

It may be observed that the effect of the second psychological law and the attitudes generated by it play an important part in maintaining schemes of co-operation known to satisfy the two principles of justice. For such schemes are liable to at least two types of instability. Instability of the first kind is present when, if any one person knows that the others will do their part, it will be worth his while not to do his: the consequences of one person's not doing his part if others do theirs may go unnoticed, or may have no ostensible effect, so that an alternative use of one's time and effort is a personal gain. Such a system of co-operation is unstable: each is tempted to depart from it if he thinks others will keep it going. Since each is aware of another's temptation, mutual trust is in danger of breaking down. Instability of the second kind is present when it is the case that if any one person knows or reasonably supposes that others will not do their part, it will be worth his while to be the first, or among the first, not to do his, or even dangerous for him not to be. These two kinds of instability are related in that if the first kind obtains, then one may think that others will not do their part, and this may bring about instability of the second kind. Where both kinds are present the scheme of co-operation is fragile and participants are moved to withdraw, or even to be afraid not to. (Disarmament schemes are subject to instability of both kinds.) Hobbes seems to have been the first to place the problem of such unstable situations at the center of the question of political obligation. One way of interpreting the Hobbesian sovereign is as an agency added to unstable systems of co-operation in such a way that it is no longer to anyone's advantage not to do his part given that others will do theirs. By keeping watch and enforcing sanctions, the sovereign acts to inhibit violations and to restore the system when violations occur; and the belief in the sovereign's efficacy removes instability of both kinds.[8]

[8] On this topic, see W. J. Baumol, *Welfare Economics and the Theory of the State* (London, 1952). Illuminating also is the discussion in R. D. Luce and H. Raiffa, *Games and Decisions* (New York, 1957), ch. v.

Now relations of friendship and mutual trust have a similar effect. Once a system of co-operation satisfying the stated conditions is set up and a period of uncertainty survived, the passage of time renders it more stable, given an evident intention on the part of all to do their part. The generation of feelings of friendship and mutual trust tends to reinforce the scheme of co-operation. A greater temptation is required and, should violations occur, the feelings of guilt, shown in wishing to make reparation and the like, will tend to restore the broken relations. Thus not only may such a system of co-operation be stable in the sense that when each man thinks the others will do their part there is no tendency for him not to do his; it may be inherently stable in the sense that the persistence of the scheme generates, in accordance with the second psychological law, inclinations which further support it. The effect, then, of relations of friendship and mutual trust is analogous to the role of the sovereign; only in this case it is the consequence of a certain psychological principle of human nature in such systems, and of the implications of the generated attitudes.

V

The third part of the psychological construction concerns principle guilt. In both the previous forms of guilt I have supposed it to be connected with an actual natural attitude toward certain particular persons: with authority guilt these persons are parents, and in association guilt they are fellow-associates. Very often, however, we feel guilty for doing something when those injured or put at a disadvantage are not persons with whom we are tied by any form of particular fellow-feeling. To account for feelings of guilt of this kind—principle guilt—I assume a third psychological law as follows: given that the attitudes of love and trust, friendly feelings and mutual respect, have been generated in accordance with the two previous psychological laws, then, if a person (and his associates) are the beneficiaries of a successful and enduring institution or scheme of co-operation known to satisfy the two principles of justice, he will acquire a sense of justice. This will show itself in at least two ways: first, in an acceptance of those particular institutions which are just (as defined by the two principles) and from which he and his associates have benefited. This acceptance of particular institutions shows itself in feeling guilty for infractions which harm other persons even though these persons are not the objects of any particular fellow-feelings. It may be that they have not yet had sufficient opportunity to show an evident intention of doing their part, and so are not yet the object of such feelings by the second law. Or it may be that the institution is too large to allow occasion for such particular ties to be established. The sense of justice will manifest itself second in a willingness to work for (or at least not to oppose) the setting up of just institutions, or for the reform of existing ones where justice requires it. Guilt feelings associated with the sense of justice are characterized as principle guilt feelings since in their explanation reference is made to principles, in this case to principles of justice. These principle guilt feelings spring from breaches of institutions accepted as satisfying the principles of justice, or from resistance to reforms which these principles are seen to require.

Principle guilt is, then, connected with the acceptance of the principles of justice. It represents a step beyond the understanding of their derivation which is all that is presupposed by association guilt. One might say that principle guilt is guilt proper. It is, as the two previous forms of guilt were not, a complete moral feeling. For this reason authority and association guilt should be spoken of with the prefixed adjective. They are not, as defined, complete moral feelings although they include many of the characteristic aspects of moral feelings. Once the full development to principle guilt has taken place, however, and the principles of justice which specify the conditions of association guilt are accepted, then the infractions which gave rise to association guilt will be guilt proper; for now the reference to the accepted principle is given in a person's explanation of his feeling. Furthermore, where the ties of natural attitudes are present in the form of friendship and mutual trust, the feelings of guilt will be greater than where they are absent. The transmuted association guilt will reinforce principle guilt. If one assumes that an appropriate guilt feeling—that is, one based on true beliefs concerning what one has done—implies a fault, and that a greater feeling of guilt implies a greater fault, one can infer that conduct giving rise to association guilt feelings is wrong. Thus all the violations of the natural attitudes generated by association— in particular friendship, affection, and mutual trust—are wrong.

The sense of justice helps to maintain schemes of co-operation just as the natural attitudes of friendship and trust do. The acceptance of the principles of justice implies, failing a special explanation, an avoidance of their violation and a recognition that advantages gained in conflict with them are without value; and should such violations nevertheless occur, in cases of temptation, feelings of guilt will tend to restore joint activity. To grasp this fact, one has only to consider the variety of inclinations and inhibitions in which these feelings are expressed. A system in which each person has, and is known by everyone to have, a sense of justice is inherently stable. Other things being equal, the forces making for its stability increase as time passes. (It may nevertheless break down at a later time if outside elements make for increasingly greater temptations.) This inherent stability is a direct consequence of the reciprocal relation between the second and third psychological laws. The psychological construction as a whole is consistent and self-reinforcing: it is intrinsically stable. To explain this properly one would have to bring the institutions constituting the setting for authority guilt under the regulation of the principles of justice, but there is no insuperable difficulty in this.[9]

[9] Sections VI–VIII have been omitted.

Bibliography

For each of the authors included, the natural place to begin is with the work from which the excerpt is taken. The following list indicates for each selection additional material which may be of interest.

PLATO
Apology, Crito, Protagoras, Euthyphro, Meno. [Short dialogues dealing with ethical problems.] A. W. H. Adkins, *Merit and Responsibility.* Oxford: Clarendon Press, 1960, Chaps. XI and XIV. [A study of the development of the concept of moral responsibility in Greek thought from Homer to Aristotle.]

JOHN CALVIN
Compare selections from Calvin with those of St. Augustine in A. I. Melden (ed.), *Ethical Theories: A Book of Readings.* Englewood Cliffs, N.J.: Prentice-Hall, Inc., 1955. R. H. Tawney, *Religion and the Rise of Capitalism.* New York: Penguin Books, 1947, Chap. II.

ALBERT CAMUS
The Stranger. New York: Vintage Books, 1958. [Camus's first novel.] Walter Kaufman (ed.), *Existentialism from Dostoyevsky to Sartre.* New York: Meridian Books, 1958. [A collection of short and relatively nontechnical passages from the works of existential thinkers.]

THOMAS HOBBES
Leviathan (Parts I and II) H. Schneider (ed.). New York: Liberal Arts Press, 1958. R. S. Peters, *Hobbes,* Baltimore: Penguin Books, 1956.

JEAN-JACQUES ROUSSEAU
E. Cassirer, *Rousseau, Kant, Goethe.* New York: Harper & Row, 1963.

EARL OF SHAFTESBURY
D. Daiches Raphael, *The Moral Sense.* Oxford: Clarendon Press, 1947.

IMMANUEL KANT
Foundations of the Metaphysics of Morals: What is Enlightenment? Lewis White Beck (trans.). New York: Liberal Arts Press, 1956. H. J. Paton, *The Categorical Imperative.* Chicago: University of Chicago Press, 1949.

JOHN STUART MILL
Autobiography. Oxford: Clarendon Press, 1940. [Compare selections from Bentham in Melden, *op. cit.*] G. E. Moore, *Ethics.* Oxford: Claren-

don Press, 1912, Chaps. 1 and 2. [A clear and systematic exposition of the utilitarian position.]

ARISTOTLE
W. D. Ross, *Aristotle*. New York: Meridian Books, 1963. J. H. Randall, Jr., *Aristotle*. New York: Columbia University Press, 1963. Adkins, *op. cit.*, Chaps. XV and XVI.

JOHN RAWLS
"Justice as Fairness," *Philosophical Review*, LXVII (1958).